TRENDS PERFECT
KITCHEN

TRENDS PERFECT KITCHEN

Sunset

Sunset

Sunset Books
80 Willow Road
Menlo Park, CA 94025

www.sunset.com

Trends *Perfect Kitchen* is produced in association with:
Trends Publishing International, Auckland, New Zealand.
www.trendsideas.com

Publisher: David Johnson
Editorial Director: Paul Taylor
Trends Home Series Editor: Rachel Galyer
Associate Editor: Kelli Robson
Production Director: Louise Messer
Editorial Administrator: Kate Ballinger

Chief Executive Officer: John Owen
President: Terry Newell
Publisher: Lynn Humphries
Managing Editor: Angela Handley
Design Manager: Helen Perks
Editorial Coordinator: Kiren Thandi
Production Manager: Caroline Webber
Production Coordinator: James Blackman
Sales Manager: Emily Jahn
Vice President International Sales: Stuart Laurence
Series Design Concept: John Bull
Project Designer: Lena Lowe
Text: Julia Richardson

ISBN 0-376-00177-1

Cover photography
Front cover TOP LEFT Architect: Gerard Murtagh; Photographer: David Sandison. TOP
RIGHT Kitchen Designer: Kitchens by Design; Photographer: Gérald Lopez. BOTTOM LEFT
Architect: John Chaplin; Kitchen Designer: Ingrid Geldof; Photographer: Doc Ross.
BOTTOM RIGHT Architect: Diana Meckfessel; Photographer: Tim Maloney.
Spine Designer: Dorothy Street; Photographer: Lloyd Park.
Back cover TOP LEFT Architect: Chris Ralston; Photographer: Anton Curley. TOP RIGHT
Consultant: Jeff Tan, Unique Kitchen Fusion; Photographer: Peter Mealin. BOTTOM LEFT
Architect: Hedgpeth Architects; Photographer: Tim Maloney. BOTTOM RIGHT Designer:
Hardy Interiors; Photographer: Simon Kenny.

Color reproduction by SC (Sang Choy) International Pte Ltd
Printed in China by SNP Leefung Printers Limited

A Weldon Owen Production

CONTENTS

INTRODUCTION

Much is expected of the modern kitchen: it must be a reliable work space, a welcoming social venue and an aesthetic asset. Start with a floorplan that makes it possible to work comfortably, efficiently and safely, finish it in a style that suits the house and its occupants, then sit back and watch with satisfaction as it grows into its role as the social hub of the household.

❶ A neutral palette and finely detailed cabinetry are consistent with the soft elegance of the interiors throughout this house. A rustic tool hung above the sink is an edgy inclusion that gives the room a sense of character.

❶

❷ Elements such as sliding and folding doors, walls and windows can manipulate the structure of an open-plan kitchen, exposing it to surrounding living areas for everyday access or large-scale entertaining and closing it off when a more formal, controlled environment is required.

❷

PERFECT KITCHENS

There's something engagingly human about a kitchen. Its floorplan is measured by our footsteps, its efficiency judged in terms of what we might reach with an outstretched arm, its success gauged by how much time we spend there with our friends and family, whether or not we are engaged in the act of preparing a meal.

At the same time, it is a very public space. A century ago, affluent households hosted guests in stuffily overdecorated parlors. In these more casual and egalitarian times, the open-plan living area with the kitchen at its hub is the place where bank managers, mothers-in-law, business colleagues and childhood friends are entertained.

Given its personal scale and its very public face, the modern kitchen issues what might be seen as a confronting challenge: to lucidly identify our needs, our interests and our values and also to find a way of executing them not only efficiently, but also expressively.

EFFICIENCY AND EXPOSURE

With its standardized formats and conventional inclusions, the kitchen often escapes the personalized detailing of other rooms in the house, but this need not be the case. Like any other design project, the best results follow when the role of the space is analyzed in relation to the people who will use it most. Don't act on assumptions or conventions. Instead, ask yourself the questions that will reveal your kitchen customs. Do you live on a diet of salads and stir-fries and never, ever use an oven? Do you reheat take-out dinners in a microwave oven every night of the working week? Is your refrigerator merely an oversized ice box for the storage of a wedge of blue vein cheese and a bottle of semillon? If you don't need the oven, don't install it, but consider installing a hob with a wok burner. If you depend on take-out, spend up on a top-quality microwave oven and opt for a basic range. If a double-door refrigerator would be a waste, seek out a compact under-counter refrigerator and use the extra space to enlarge the pantry or extend the dining area. A kitchen that accurately meets the habits of the household will fulfill its domestic purpose with ease and be an easy and engaging space for all kinds of visitors to occupy.

The extraordinary popularity of the open-plan kitchen is a thing to be celebrated, representing as it does the revolutionary democratization of the family structure. Once a place of domestic servitude — fulfilled either by paid servants or by an unpaid housewife and mother — the kitchen is now a space for all members of the household. And with the heavy weight of duty lifted from the cook, cooking itself has flourished as a joyful, satisfying, participatory pastime.

The issue that concerns most homeowners, though, is the sheer visual exposure of the space. This is, after all, primarily a work place, yet here it is on view to the living and dining areas, perhaps even the outdoor entertaining spaces or the front door. There really are only two responses that offer any possibility of success: either camouflage the identity of the space so that it meshes with the fabric of the nearby living areas, or revel in its difference, embracing its utilitarian character and emphasizing its distinction from the recreational spaces that surround it. Anything in between is likely to look like a half-hearted attempt at either one of the extremes. The decision to opt for display or discretion is a matter of personal preference, but both strategies rely on the provision of good storage. Storage units must have the

❶

❶ Extensive built-in cabinetry and a sleek hanging-rail system satisfy the storage requirements of this kitchen and ensure that it maintains the streamlined look established in the surrounding spaces.

❷ Small details that specifically match the habits and needs of the household are the difference between a kitchen that functions only satisfactorily and one that offers a spectacularly personalized service. Here, a simple customized niche keeps the telephone close to hand without taking up valuable counter space.

❸ Luxuries such as a second sink or expanses of stainless steel or granite often earn their place in the kitchen by dramatically improving the efficiency of the space or by promising high performance and long, reliable service.

❷

❸

capacity to house their contents in an adequate and orderly fashion, whether those contents are to be concealed within sleek, wall-like expanses of unadorned cabinetry or exposed in merry farmhouse fashion with pot racks and open shelving.

ENVIRONMENT AND ECONOMY

The impact that our chosen lifestyle can have on the rest of the planet is inescapably evident in the kitchen. More than any other room in the house, the kitchen has the potential to be excessively wasteful or inspiringly efficient and responsible.

Fortunately, more and more manufacturers are developing appliances that compete in terms of environmental efficiency. Some even go so far as to consider the future recyclability of their products once their working life is over. The expensive research and development that goes into these products tends to lead to higher prices, but — as the manufacturers themselves are wont to say — some of that extra cost can be offset against savings on electricity, gas and water bills.

The efficiency of appliances is probably the most easily understood of the environmental issues in the kitchen, but there is another facet of kitchen design that has an enormous and often ignored impact on resources: the unnecessary production and consumption of kitchen fixtures. In modern society, it is common for people to move home five or six times in a lifetime. Frequently, the purchase of a new property

The first priority of kitchen planning is to create a safe, comfortable work environment. Those functional considerations are generally addressed by structure, leaving you reasonably free to be fanciful in your choice of decorative finishes and flourishes.

is closely followed by the installation of a new kitchen, yet many deficiencies of design or decoration can be put right by the adaptation of fixtures already in place, without a wholesale demolition of the existing kitchen. Clumsy floorplans can be improved by repositioning existing appliances (some will be harder to shift than others) or rearranging modular cabinetry. And if it's a matter of aesthetics, the standard sizes of fitted kitchen cabinets have made it easy to replace one set of door and drawer fronts with another in a different style.

STRUCTURE, SOCIABILITY AND SUCCESS

It's little wonder that the design of a new kitchen becomes such a preoccupation for so many homeowners; after all, it carries with it the expectations of enormous financial outlay. Yet, with optimism, those burdens become exciting possibilities. A well-designed kitchen is likely to be well used and well loved. Cooks will feel the simple pleasure of reaching out and finding a chopping knife exactly where and when it is needed. Partners will be able to prepare a meal together, talking over the day as they work. Children will have access to the things they need to organize their own breakfasts so that parents can sleep in on a Saturday morning. Teenagers will enjoy organizing their own snacks and catering for their friends after school. Friends will mill about, glass in hand, helping out by tossing a salad or grating some cheese for a dinner party. In short, a successful kitchen will be invested with the energy, animation and unstructured sociability that make a house a home.

❶

❶ A lot of thought has gone into the details in this period home. Traditional horizontal tiling and a retro grocery sign ensure this modern kitchen sits comfortably in the space.

❷ In the post-war period, an emphasis on cleanliness, technology and high efficiency meant that personal, decorative touches were often absent from the kitchen. Here, a pair of framed prints and a collection of vintage

kitchenalia do not hinder the performance of the space but contribute much in the way of character.

❸ In this handsome kitchen, the doors of an enormous pantry match the nearby interior door in terms of scale and detailing. This design tactic creates a strong link between the kitchen area and the open-plan space in which it is located.

❷

❸

OPEN-PLAN KITCHENS

An open-plan format makes the kitchen central to the life of the
household. It lets the cook see and be part of whatever is going on,
and ensures that adjoining living spaces will benefit from the warm
sense of home that emanates quite naturally from a busy kitchen.
It does, however, place on constant display an area that is essentially
a work space, so finishes must be selected with special care.

ALONE IN A CROWD

Even though it is, by definition, part of a larger, multipurpose space, an open-plan kitchen must be clearly defined, or risk looking like nothing more than a motley collection of electrical appliances in the corner of a living or dining room. In a house full of dramatic painted feature walls and soaring dimensions, this kitchen achieves distinction with its organic palette and lowered ceiling. The dropped ceiling helps to define the space, but also brings the light fittings down to a height where they will provide effective illumination for work surfaces. Hoop pine features on all vertical surfaces, giving the space a uniformity and a warmth less apparent in the more dynamic living and entertaining areas. Stainless steel is used for the primary work surfaces around the cooktop and the sink, while a striking slab of black granite tops the peninsula. The lineal dash of black is a visual link to the feature-defining black joinery used around windows and doorways throughout the house.

PREVIOUS PAGES By their very nature, open-plan kitchens tend to be a backdrop to — and a participant in — the everyday life of the household. Here, where a mosaic-tiled swimming pool laps the very walls of the house, vast panels of fixed glass ensure that the kitchen is a permanent player, even in the family's outdoor recreational life.

❶ The glazing that overlooks the pool is composed of fixed panels of glass. Natural ventilation is facilitated by the casement windows above the sink and the long, thin louvered window in the red feature wall.

❶

❷

❷ A simplified palette of materials featuring hoop pine cabinetry ensures a strong impact and helps set this kitchen apart from the surrounding living spaces.

❸ The stainless steel used for work surfaces is also applied as a backsplash and is a match for the door hardware. Black granite provides a contrast and is specifically used to link the kitchen with architectural elements elsewhere. ❸

① A quartet of canopy windows surrounds a petite portion of wall cabinetry. The frosted glass of the lower panels admits a filtered light and preserves privacy.

②

KITCHEN CORNERSTONE

Encompassing some of the most reliable principles of open-plan kitchen design, this kitchen sits inconspicuously in the corner of a large L-shaped space. Two walls of floor-to-ceiling cabinetry form a neutral backdrop to the kitchen. Color-matched to adjacent walls and finished with discreet stainless steel door hardware, the cabinets are not obviously distinguishable from the walls of the neighboring dining and living zones, yet they provide abundant storage space as well as concealing a refrigerator and a dishwasher. The island, composed of rock maple, brushbox hardwood, limestone and stainless steel, has design qualities that make it the equal of nearby freestanding furniture pieces, linking this very efficient kitchen with the living spaces that bracket it.

② The sculptural island is extremely practical in form. Its extended dimensions allow room for utilitarian kitchen storage on one side, while storage for tableware is accessible on the outer facade.

③ The way that the vertical panel of brushbox hardwood pierces the limestone countertop is highly theatrical, yet it serves two functional purposes. It creates a slim overhang, defining a casual eating area on the outer edge of the island, and it screens the kitchen's primary work surface from the nearby living spaces. ③

At a Stretch

Open-plan kitchens can make the most of their loosely defined boundaries by taking advantage of neighboring spaces, with features such as additional storage space on adjacent walls. That's what has been achieved in this long, narrow kitchen with a wall of cabinetry stretching all the way out into the dining area. The approach is successful only because the cabinets don't look like standard kitchen storage space and therefore don't seem out of place as a backdrop to the dining table. At the point where the space moves from kitchen zone to dining zone, the cabinetry deftly switches from a stainless steel work surface to a discreet white laminate surface, while the door hardware changes from easy-to-grab door handles to elegant drawer pulls. Display niches backed by sandblasted glass complete the artful deception.

The slope of the ceiling necessitated the installation of a lighting bulkhead that would bring the lights closer to the surfaces they were intended to illuminate. Feature lighting on the top side of the panel emphasizes the sweeping height of the ceiling.

① The kitchen and living areas are bisected by a staircase. An internal window makes a visual connection between the two spaces and allows the kitchen to benefit from the natural light entering the interior through the huge skylight that sits above the staircase. A granite counter acts as a transition element between the elegantly furnished living spaces and the hardworking stainless steel work surfaces along the back wall.

② The exterior wall of the house that borders the kitchen and dining spaces overlooks a neighbor's property. In search of light, but keen to maintain privacy, the architect installed panels of sandblasted glass. Set into display niches, the panels also serve as stylish backgrounds for a varied art collection.

❶ An angled ceiling gives an impression of roominess in a narrow galley kitchen. A skylight supplies the far end of the room with its own source of natural light.

❷ A panel by the sink hides a dishwasher. The door fronts beyond the wall oven conceal a refrigerator. The cooktop, surrounded by a stainless steel countertop, sits inconspicuously against the backdrop of a stainless steel backsplash. This visual discretion means that the kitchen — highly visible from the dining area — tends not to stand out as a work space.

❶   ❷

FREEWHEELING STYLE

Rarely is an open-plan kitchen located right in the middle of the house with no full-height walls of its own, but that is the case in this extraordinary refurbishment. The artful space makes the most of its center-stage location, taking on a role as a sculptural showpiece as well as a working kitchen. A curved wall is the space's most distinctive feature, yet it serves a practical purpose, too, sweeping from the counter-height expected in an open-plan kitchen to the full height required for the positioning of tall items, such as the refrigerator. The wall is paneled in wood, an echo of the house's exterior. An economical laminate was chosen for the cabinetry. A pale, streaked, wood look-alike, it is a tonal match for the wood used on the wall, and makes a connection with the wooden floors used throughout the house.

❶ The curved partition wall begins at the point in the counter where the cooktop is located. The wall — clad here with stainless steel — is high enough to function as a backsplash, containing potentially messy splashes and splatters.

❶

❷ The independent structure of the kitchen made it possible to alter the floorplan of this 1970s-era house without obliterating its distinctive and appealing characteristics, including tall walls of glazing and a wood-lined, sloping ceiling.

❷

❶ The spiraling, wraparound partition wall accentuates the angular shape of the room and serves as a backing to tall storage units and a refrigerator. A separate island is positioned away from the wall, completing the loose shell-like shape of the kitchen and permitting unencumbered views of the ocean.

❷ The wall was designed in such a way that the stainless steel counter extends as a ridge around the outer surface of the kitchen. Given the kitchen's location close to the entrance, this shelf becomes a useful and accessible repository for keys, mail and those other small, but essential trappings of daily life for which house plans and decorating schemes often fail to allot space. The textured surface will conceal the scratches and fingermarks that are so visible on a sheer stainless steel surface.

ON DISPLAY

Open-plan kitchens frequently have limited wall space, reducing the amount of wall-hung cabinetry that can be used to provide storage. The solution for this storage-starved, open-plan space was to suspend a bank of cabinets over the island that separates the kitchen from the nearby dining area. The cabinets are faced on both sides by glass-fronted doors, making the contents accessible from either side and reducing the visual obstruction so that the free-flowing character of the space is maintained. Extra reinforcement was required in the ceiling to support the weight of the cabinets.

Fronted on both sides by framed glass doors and lined with clear glass shelves, the ceiling-mounted cabinetry was designed to minimize visual disruption. Wall-hung cabinets elsewhere in the kitchen also feature framed glass doors. The use of glass alleviates the sense of enclosure in what is really quite a narrow space, while the textured finish of those panels partially reveals but shields the contents within.

❶

❶ The high visibility of open-plan kitchens leaves two courses of action: either conceal the identity of the space with subtle finishes and integrated appliances, or make a showpiece of it with eye-catching detail. The latter approach is followed here, particularly in the installation of an extravagantly veined marble backsplash behind the range.

❷ One of the aims in creating this new kitchen was to pay respect to the Georgian architecture of the house without necessarily subjugating the design to traditional forms. The recessed panels of the drawer and door fronts are a reference to Georgian style, as is the symmetrical layout of the space. A black toeboard below the cabinetry is matched by a strip of black marble that runs around the wall at counter height. These bands accentuate the woodwork and create the illusion that the cabinetry is wall hung, visually "lifting" the cabinets off the floor.

❷

At the Front Line

Open-plan kitchens must always be designed with an eye to style as well as function, given that they are far more exposed to scrutiny than kitchens housed in separate rooms. This issue was all the more relevant for this kitchen, situated just inside the front door and immediately visible to anyone entering the house. An island designed to have the look of a solid piece of furniture is the space's centerpiece. It has a dramatic presence in the room, drawing attention away from the necessary functionality of the rest of the space. It also acts as a physical screen. Together, the raised servery counter, the wooden end panels and the suspended, glass-fronted cabinet successfully conceal from view the messiest areas of this working kitchen.

❶ A decision was made to give this kitchen a bold presence that distracted from its utilitarian purpose. Planes of opaque glass, wood, and black and off-white laminates establish a graphic look.

❷ An overhead cabinet faced with opaque glass and suspended between the wooden end panels helps to contain the kitchen neatly without enclosing the space too much.

❸ Black laminate clads the full-height pantry and the housing of the refrigerator, forming distinctive, contrasting columns that echo the structure of the wood-framed island.

SHIP SHAPE

Approached with optimism, the awkward angles of a space can become a feature of its design. Here, a sink and cooktop have been set into the counter that runs along under the sloping ceiling. Windows have been installed in the ceiling and in the wall directly below it. These windows form a kind of cut-out, opening up these hardworking areas to fresh air and daylight and creating an alfresco work zone. The jaunty angle of the ceiling and the seaside location of the house set up a nautical mood, which is complemented by the smart, streamlined look of stainless steel door hardware set flush into metallic, midnight blue cabinetry.

Though part of an open-plan area, it was not the owners' intention that this kitchen should be readily visible from the main living areas. A curving island bar orients the space so that it faces away from those recreational areas, although it is within easy reach of the dining area. To the extent that it is exposed to view, the kitchen's presence is camouflaged by the use of wood veneer on the outer facade and end pieces of the island. The veneer is a match for that used on cabinetry installed elsewhere in this open-plan space.

❶

❶ Glazing in the wall and the ceiling showers the work areas with an abundance of natural light and also plays a part in alleviating the sense of enclosure often caused by a steeply sloping ceiling.

❷ The use of wood veneer as a backsplash material is highly unusual. A super-fine sheet of real wood, veneer is not a very robust surface. It provides an interesting textural element to the kitchen, however, and makes a visual connection with cabinetry used throughout the space. Around the cooktop and sink, a switch is made to a more durable stainless steel backsplash.

❷

MID-CENTURY MODULAR

In keeping with the rest of the original fixtures of this 1950s-era house, this kitchen refurbishment was designed to have a streamlined, modular look. The back wall of cabinetry incorporates an integrated refrigerator and a pantry, yet its virtually featureless surface — interrupted only by the most discreet of door handles and accented by a set of display shelves — gives the impression of a solid wooden backdrop. Matching wooden shutters, window frames and counter stools add to the sleek uniformity of the space. A stainless steel countertop with integrated sink makes a visual link to the stainless steel appliances. A granite breakfast bar provides a punchy contrast and is a fitting choice of material, given the house's location on the face of an old quarry.

❶ Sliding windows were installed above the counter to make the most of the warm air and fresh breezes in this appealingly temperate area. Matching sliding wooden screens can be adjusted as necessary throughout the day to counteract glare on the stainless steel work surface.

❶

❷ A series of folding windows was fitted above the counter on the wall that overlooks a sunny garden. The retractable windows allow the work surface to function as a servery for the outdoor area.

❷

In Full View

Removing walls and installing internal windows made it possible for this kitchen to benefit from the light sources and ocean views of the adjacent living and dining areas, but it also left the room exposed from many different angles. The owners' aim, therefore, was to create a sleek, simple kitchen that could withstand the scrutiny. Cabinetry located beneath the stainless steel work surfaces was clad in a metallic gray laminate and interspersed with stainless steel appliances, a monochromatic approach that distinguishes the primary work zone. Floor-to-ceiling cabinets on the wall closest to the living space were finished with a lighter color in keeping with the palette of the rooms beyond.

❶ Although the kitchen is partially screened from nearby formal spaces, it remains fully exposed to casual living and dining areas. A subdued, monochrome palette played out in metallic gray cabinetry and stainless steel countertops camouflages stainless steel appliances, fittings and accessories, thereby reducing the visual impact of the work space.

❷ Folding doors retract fully, transforming the work surfaces around the sink into a servery that caters to the courtyard's outdoor table setting.

❸ The broad countertop of an internal window can be used to display fresh flowers to brighten up both the kitchen and the adjacent formal living areas, but its functional depth also makes it an ideal servery when entertaining on a large scale.

1 An internal window, surrounded by cabinetry, was included primarily so that the kitchen could benefit from the ocean views visible through the living area's windows. The reverse view from the formal living area through to the courtyard beyond the kitchen is another advantage. A broad countertop means that the window can also function as a servery for the dining area.

2 A U-shaped installation of cabinetry efficiently houses the main work sites of the kitchen with just a few short steps between the sink, the refrigerator and the range. The partnering of the stainless steel work surfaces and the metallic gray laminate of the cabinetry makes for an outstandingly practical work area, one that is unlikely to betray the minute-to-minute spills and splashes of the kitchen. The monochromatic approach also sets this apart as the functional zone of an open-plan space.

2

COUNTRY KITCHENS

Traditionally, the farmhouse kitchen is a room in which business and household matters, family, workmates and guests all share equal footing. When we re-create the look in the city, in the suburbs or by the sea, we embrace the warmth, hospitality, informality and good, old-fashioned common sense of the country kitchen.

FANCY FREE

The best country kitchens are characterized by a lack of pretension: materials appear in their simplest form, everyday items are stored precisely where they will be needed and no attempt is made to mask the presence of big, functional pieces such as the range and the refrigerator. Built as an addition to a historic house, this kitchen embodies those notions. All the countertops were selected to perform specific tasks: the marble surface is for pastry making, the butcher's block is for chopping and the robust stainless steel surrounding the sink is the ideal surface for dirty dishes. No superfluous decoration in the form of paint finishes or soft furnishings is required, because elements such as the American oak cabinetry, the raw sandstone of what was once the back wall of the house and the sandstone flooring have inherent tones and patterns that give the space its visual texture.

PREVIOUS PAGES An addition to a historic house, this kitchen confidently blends old and new. The original sandstone wall and classic tiling evoke 19th-century farmhouse style, while custom-made cabinets and stainless steel appliances stake a claim for the 21st century's emphasis on high performance.

❶ The sandstone wall would not have been at all suitable as a backsplash for the range. Sandstone is a porous material and, in this case, is particularly rough in texture: it would have absorbed every particle of grime and bead of moisture and no amount of scrubbing would ever have coaxed it clean again. A broad strip of moisture-resistant, easy-to-clean tiles does the job very competently. Their rectangular shape and the brick-like pattern in which they are laid are typical of the period in which the house was built and serve to connect the original house with this new extension.

❶ Country living means doing without a corner shop or a local supermarket. As a result, occasional shopping trips yield vast quantities of tinned and packaged food items. In this house, a separate pantry was a necessity rather than a luxury. Shelves were kept narrow so that jars, bottles and boxes were easy to see at a glance and therefore less likely to be forgotten and possibly wasted. A comfortably deep counter provides ample space for the unpacking of shopping bags and can be used as an extra work surface when the kitchen is crowded. So, too, can the mobile work trolley.

❷ Although it has the streamlined look of a modular, built-in kitchen, the work areas here are in fact composed of freestanding units. All have stainless steel frames and American oak shelves, doors and drawer fronts, but are finished off with a variety of different countertops, including stainless steel, butcher's block wood and marble. The advantage of using freestanding pieces is that they can be reconfigured or even moved to a new house sometime down the track. They also hark back to the traditional, unfitted format of the classic farmhouse kitchen.

REAL-LIFE RUSTIC

A kitchen in the country doesn't have to be a cliché-cluttered space of cottage chairs and wicker baskets, as this kitchen proves. The colors of the surrounding landscape establish this kitchen's rural character, while the materials selected are suitably rugged: concrete for the countertop and the floor, steel for the remaining work surfaces, and corrugated metal cladding for the island. Cabinets are faced with wood stained in rich, earthy tones, an approach that continues the rustic theme, but adds an element of visual sophistication to give the space a contemporary edge.

❶ The direction of the wood grain, the color of the stain and the style of the door hardware alternate from panel to panel in the multi-doored island. It's a complex and labor-intensive mode of construction, but the result is a feature piece that defines the kitchen's character.

❷ The wood-faced staircase picks up on the angular geometry established by the corrugated steel and reinforced by the zigzag door handles. Also striking a graphic punch are the deep windowsills in the exterior wall, their dimensions emphasized by a rich, chocolaty paint color.

❷

❶

① Cooktops located on islands offer great opportunities for cooks to mix with guests or other family members, but present problems in terms of ventilation. Hoods can be ceiling mounted, but they cause a massive obstruction to sightlines in an open-plan kitchen. Here, ventilation requirements are met by four hooded stainless steel vents, tucked away in the wall of a raised servery.

② Concrete was selected as a countertop for the island partly because its rugged good looks suit the style of the kitchen, but also because it can be shaped to almost any form, including the sweeping curve shown here.

③ Zigzag and wave-shaped handles make more of an impact when side by side with simple, cylindrical drawer pulls.

④ Concrete flooring was given a terra-cotta stain, then polished and buffed for a refined finish. The resulting surface is durable, easy to clean and eminently practical in a hard-working space such as a kitchen, but it also evokes the rich earth of the land on which the house is built. The concrete of the island countertop was tinted with a black stain, then polished and buffed in the same manner as the floor for a low-maintenance, waterproof finish.

AN ELEGANT TRANSFER

This genteel kitchen proves that widely ranging decorative influences can be drawn together to form a composed and coherent space. Some of the details — the false mantel and the molding of the cabinet doors, for example — were dictated by the architectural style of the Victorian house in which the kitchen is located. The exposed hinges of the cabinetry are a trademark of Provençal style, a look much favored by the widely traveled owners. The color scheme was set by the handpainted Portuguese tiles, collected by the owners over many years. These tiles were arranged in a deliberately loose fashion to mask the inconsistency of the collection. If there is one unifying element to these disparately sourced features, it is that they all represent the owners' cherished passions.

❶ The ventilation unit is concealed within a false mantel, a replica of an original fireplace located elsewhere in the house.

❷ Soft furnishings are an uncommon sight in modern kitchens. Here, a roman blind contributes to the delicate character of the room.

❸ From the living room, the island's storage capacity is concealed behind elegant cabinetry, but the side facing the range gives access to pots and pans. The island's countertop is used as a servery. The owners specified that it be sized to comfortably accommodate eight dinner plates.

COUNTRY COMFORT

When restoring a period home, it's possible to install a kitchen that is true to the spirit of the place without being a slavish copy of an outmoded style. Start by identifying elements with a contemporary resonance, and find ways of introducing them into the design of a new kitchen. In this refurbishment, the wood paneling of the original cottage walls was preserved and replicated in the newly built portions of the space. The simple framework of the new cabinetry is styled after the doors of a vintage dresser. The dresser itself was installed in the dining room behind the kitchen and modified to include a servery window between the two spaces. The countertops are granite, a high-performance work surface favored in modern kitchens, but retain a traditional wooden aspect courtesy of rimu hardwood edging strips. Rimu hardwood was chosen to match the wood of the original, restored rimu floor.

❶ A vintage dresser was modified to house a servery window, linking the kitchen and the neighboring dining room. A blue cabinet with perforated steel door panels recalls the style of traditional country meat safes with their wooden frames and wire-mesh sides.

❶

❷ Open storage is a practical pleasure, keeping all the frequently used items close at hand and up off the work surfaces. It also helps to set the no-nonsense tone that is characteristic of country kitchens.   ❷

❶ The hood is centered over the range, but the pot rack pays no heed to symmetry, stretching right across the wall to maximize storage capacity. Horizontal wall tiles, typical of the era, provide an unobtrusive, though authentic, style link with the cottage's origins.

❷ Cabinetry has been designed to complement the architectural character of the cottage. Open shelves and shelving niches leave the wood paneling of the wall exposed, while the mellow mustard tone of the cabinets summons up the 1920s vintage of the house.

❷

REFINED RUSTIC

A truly traditional rustic Mediterranean kitchen would be furnished with an assortment of freestanding pieces: tables, cabinets, pantries and basins. It's an appealing look, but impractical for a contemporary kitchen where modern appliances are to be installed. Here, the effect is re-created with built-in cabinetry, affording the owners the trouble-free installation and guaranteed low maintenance of a fitted kitchen. Some of the materials, such as the simple laminated countertop, are undeniably practical and economical, but the small details — the patterned tiles of the cooktop backsplash, the decorative woodwork under the island countertop and around the hood, and the ornate iron door handles and drawer pulls — give the kitchen its charm. Twelve-inch (30-cm) terra-cotta floor tiles have been laid with unusually wide spacing, resulting in broader, more recognizable lines of grouting. The look recalls something of the rough and ready character of the Mediterranean kitchens on which it is modeled.

 An open shelf mounted below a wall cabinet provides easy access to items that are used, washed and replaced many times a day. Modest details such as this can have a huge impact on the usability of a kitchen.

❶

❷

❷ Plate racks recall the traditional furnishings of a country kitchen and serve a functional purpose, keeping plates and serving dishes close to the cooktop and oven.

❸ Economical materials, including white tiles and basic laminate, leave room in the budget for personal touches such as the handpainted tiles behind the cooktop and the hand-forged door hardware.

THE COUNTRY MANNER

Having built a new house in the style of an English country manor, the owners then set about detailing a kitchen to match. The tongue-and-groove paneling on the end pieces of the cabinetry and the walls of the island, the molding on the door fronts, the turned wooden knobs and the mullioned glass panels of the wall-mounted cabinets are all classic features of the warm but stately English country kitchen. A frieze used above the refrigerator and on the rangehood is a copy of an Irish frieze collected by the owners. A cream wash was applied to the surface of the pine cabinets, giving the kitchen an intrinsic glow that is only enhanced by an enviable supply of natural light. High-quality granite countertops were a must for these enthusiastic cooks. The granite's forest-green tone is picked up in the green and white checkerboard border of the backsplash and in the finely striped wallpaper that unites the kitchen with the adjacent family dining area. Basket drawers for table linen, a plate rack above the microwave oven and plenty of open shelving for cookbooks and tableware give the kitchen a snug and homely ambiance despite its impressive size.

❶ Lighting requirements vary throughout a kitchen. Here, a trio of fixed pendant lights, hung low over the island, and a series of ceiling-mounted downlights, set around the perimeter of the kitchen, provide clear and bright illumination for the work surfaces. A shaded chandelier brings ambient light to the dining area.

❶

❷ Decorative door fronts made by fixing pasta and candy behind glass are an inexpensive way of creating a very idiosyncratic feature, introducing an expression of modernity and individuality in an otherwise traditional space. ❷

❶

❶ The stepped-down wood and granite counter at one end of the island was specifically designed as a surface for pastry making. It's a happy bonus that the lower height also makes it the ideal work surface for children preparing their own meals.

❷ It doesn't contain any of the major appliances, but this island is clearly the hub of the kitchen. A rinsing sink and a power outlet for small appliances equip it well for most food-preparation tasks. At the end closest to the casual eating area, storage for table linen and dinnerware makes this an ideal point from which to serve meals. An overhang creates room for a couple of stools, where kitchen helpers — or spectators — can comfortably perch.

A WARM WELCOME

Sometimes a traditional approach to kitchen design is an aesthetic preference; sometimes it's a climatic necessity. Situated in a mountainous region, where temperatures frequently drop below freezing point, this ranch kitchen was built around a hefty range. The range burns day and night throughout the coldest parts of the year, heating the whole house as well as servicing the kitchen. The construction and finishes used throughout the space replicate those of the ranch's hundred-year-old outbuildings. Recycled, rough-sawed oak floorboards and a buckskin-toned plaster finish on the walls establish an aged ambiance. Metal sheeting, used on the backsplashes and cabinetry, was acid-washed to achieve a weathered finish. Even the jars containing sugar and cereals, the pottery dishes and the odds and ends of vintage kitchenware contribute to the heritage look of this brand-new space.

❶ Storage nooks crafted from thick-cut wood have a suitably rugged charm and prove themselves abundantly useful, housing a large collection of tableware.

❷ Pull-out cutting boards are installed below the top drawer of the base units throughout the kitchen. The additional work surfaces are positioned at a height that makes them easy for children to use. The horizontal strip of wood formed by the cutting boards, noticeable in among the metal-clad drawers and door fronts, is balanced by the wooden capping above the backsplash.

❸ Recessed ceiling lights are an indication of the kitchen's true vintage, but the fixtures and finishes suggest a traditional ranch.

A hanging rack, used to keep pots, pans and other commonly used bits and pieces at the ready, also contains fixtures that provide task lighting for the work surface below. Just as importantly, the pot-hung rack contributes to the country kitchen charm of the space.

This deftly designed and daintily finished kitchen works with the hundred-year-old house's original features, including some handsome architraving.

❷

TAILOR MADE

A large, well-equipped kitchen is an avid cook's dream, but it can look overwhelmingly utilitarian, particularly in the context of an open-plan space. This kitchen avoids visual dominance by incorporating finishes that blend with the architectural style of the house and with the furnishings of the adjacent dining area. It is fitted with everything the cooking enthusiast could possibly desire, including a work island with a rinsing sink, a microwave oven, vegetable baskets, a slide-out mini-pantry, and pull-out shelves big enough to store large dishes and platters. At the same time, traditional features — such as a fireplace, a beautiful bay window, patterned wallpaper with complementary curtains, and tailored cabinets that conceal the major appliances — camouflage the room's functionality.

Elegantly detailed cabinetry is the key to the success of this space. It is the stylistic link between the old house and the new kitchen, and it literally conceals the most obtrusive of the modern appliances. The double oven has the appearance of a traditional range, but the refrigerator, hood and dishwasher are integrated into the cabinetry.

❶ On the wall running perpendicular to the island, next to the feature fireplace, another piece of cabinetry serves as a "baking center." The cabinet holds appliances, including a bread-maker, and an impressive collection of cookbooks. A granite countertop is an ideal surface for pastry making.

❷ The aim was to make this a discreet kitchen, one that jarred neither with the century-old architecture of the original house nor with the graceful, garden-themed dining area nearby. A green and white palette, evident in the fabric of the upholstered dining chairs, the window dressings, the wallpaper and even some of the glazed ceramics, unifies the two zones and in so doing gently reaffirms the kitchen's place in this classically tailored house.

❸ Open storage, so characteristic of country kitchens, is in evidence here. A simple kit of utensils hangs from a rail fixed to the backsplash above the range. Slatted sliding shelves on the left-hand side house pots and pans. A ledge directly behind the range brings the unit out flush with the surrounding cabinetry and is used as a place to set fresh herbs and bottles of oil.

❶

❶ Clever planning is obvious everywhere in this kitchen. A coffee machine has been located next to the main sink and below a wall-mounted china cabinet, so that morning coffees can be made without encroaching on the main food-preparation area of the island.

❷ The island is the central area for food preparation, with basket drawers serving as a well-ventilated storage place for fresh produce. The inclusion here of a microwave oven and a rinsing sink means that the island can also function as a separate work station, where one family member can quickly heat up a meal and pour a drink without getting in the way of the cook. A raised servery screens the work surfaces around the main kitchen sink from the dining area.

BIG IDEAS

A fresh start and an abundance of space gave the owners of this new home the opportunity to realize the kitchen of their dreams. All the major appliances, the main sink and the extensive storage space are arranged around the two external walls, while one long, curving island separates the kitchen from the living areas beyond. The countertop of this island incorporates a rinsing sink, and it is broad enough for use as a breakfast bar even while food preparation is in full swing. Another island serves the cooktop and oven, providing storage for pots and pans on one side, cookbooks on the other, and a granite countertop on which to rest piping-hot dishes.

❶ The advantage that glass doors have over solid doors is that the contents of the cabinet can be seen at a glance. In this instance, they also make a more suitable match for the large window beside which they are arranged.

❷ The space incorporates three zones: at the rear, the kitchen, in the middle, a living area, and in the foreground, a dining room.

❸ This kitchen has an abundance of counter space. The areas to either side of the cooktop provide a resting place for ingredients ready to be added to the pot. Most of the food is prepared on the central island. The curved island is used primarily as a breakfast bar.

❶ Shelves in the central island hold a small library of cookbooks. Their location close to the main food-preparation area is practical, but might be considered a luxury in a kitchen with less storage space.

❷ The decision to make the outer counter an island rather than a peninsula created an opening between the kitchen and the nearby informal dining nook.

❶

❷

A GRAND DECEPTION

Showing all the signs of centuries of fond use, this rustic kitchen is in fact only a few years old. Enamored of the well-worn charms of 17th-century farmhouse kitchens, the owners set about re-creating the look with a series of artful deceptions. The salvaged, wooden ceiling beams were whitewashed, then rubbed with soot, to give the impression of age, while the solid oak cabinets were built with hand-forged hinges and nails and finished off with punched zinc inlays that were acid-washed for an antique look. The fireplace was fashioned from concrete and covered with tinted plaster, then chipped and cut to look like an old stone hearth. A stainless steel range and hood are on show and a dishwasher is integrated into cabinetry beside the sink, but all other modern appliances, including the refrigerator, are tucked into an adjacent scullery.

The majestic hearth was an essential part of the owners' plan to re-create a 17th-century farmhouse kitchen and is now the centerpiece of the room. Its raised construction allows for a clever wood-storage system. Firewood, collected outdoors, is bundled into baskets then pushed into the tailor-made slot below the fireplace via floor-level doors in the exterior wall. Ash from the hearth is removed in a similar manner, being swept into the baskets and pushed back outside through the doors for disposal.

❶ This kitchen illustrates how newly made products can be used to create a delightfully old-fashioned space. The diamond-paned leaded glass windows, the lever-handled faucet sets and the deep porcelain sink were all bought new. A more authentic alternative would have been to search for original materials, but these reproductions guarantee the high performance and ease of installation associated with modern building products.

❶

❷ Salvaged wood features throughout the kitchen, gracing the space with its well-worn charm. The lintels over the windows were once railroad ties, while Oregon wood from demolition sites was used to fashion the ceiling beams and the work surface of the island. The legs of the island were made from jarrah hardwood.

❷

3

URBAN KITCHENS

Urban kitchens take their cue from the city's professional kitchen workspaces. They are hardworking, hardwearing rooms that never seek to conceal their purpose or dress up their functioning parts. Everything about them is high performance: the surfaces, the fixtures and the appliances. And it's all there, on show and ready to use, whatever the time of day or night.

GENERATIONAL CHANGE

This kitchen tackles one of refurbishing's most difficult challenges: how to give a space a contemporary identity in a way that doesn't jar with the architecture of the original house. Here, tones, textures and forms that evoke the 1970s era in which the house was built are treated in a way that produces a strong contemporary aesthetic. The honey-toned wooden cabinetry is long and low, with milled door handles and drawer pulls typical of the period. Glass features on cabinet doors and walls, giving the room a low-key glamour accented by the sheen of stainless steel. The kitchen and the adjacent outdoor pool area are separated by a wall of pivoting glass doors. When the doors are swung open, the two spaces become a single indoor-outdoor area. The wood-lined ceiling and the wash-down character of the ceramic-tiled floor recall poolside shelters, setting the tone for a laid-back city lifestyle.

PREVIOUS PAGES The backpainted glass of the backsplash is also used as a wall treatment throughout the kitchen. The look is light, ethereal and very modern, and complements the kitchen's poolside setting. Cabinetry is cantilevered, so no supporting legs are required, leaving the cabinets to float against a backdrop of pale, luminous glass.

❶ Decorative steel grilles above the exterior doors are a relocated, but original feature of the 1970s-era house and provide a useful style reference. The long horizontal lines and clean-cut corners of the kitchen play on that lean, spare aesthetic.

A Different Drum

Generous use of stainless steel and some innovative shapes and textures give a sense of industry to this very roomy kitchen. The distinctive island counter sits atop two steel drums, one of which houses plumbing for a rinsing sink while the other supports a circular cutting block. A textured stainless steel countertop features on the island, but wood was chosen for the peninsula counter, providing a warmer surface suitable for the family's children to use when doing their homework or grabbing an after-school snack. Despite some very unconventional elements, this kitchen sits comfortably in a relaxed family home. Extensive wooden cabinetry and blocks of solid color represent more familiar kitchen finishes and prevent the space from becoming too forbidding.

❶ The starting point for this unique design was the need to house plumbing to the rinsing sink. The effect, though, is like a flash of lightning in a gleaming, industrially influenced space.

❶

❷

❷ The designer opted to make the third supporting leg used in the kitchen a cone, as a trio of steel drums would have given the room an unwelcome heaviness.

❸ The stainless steel used on the island would have been uncomfortably cold on the peninsula, where the children sit to do their homework. Wood is a smart choice, since it also performs well as a work surface. ❸

❶ High-grade appliances and extensive storage facilities, such as the twin pull-out pantries that flank the double-door refrigerator, signal the serious intentions of this kitchen. That sobriety is countered by the cheerful — even whimsical — shapes and forms of the island and the peninsula.

❷ Empty spaces below the peninsula and the island create a sense of openness in the kitchen. The tapering, cone-shaped leg of the peninsula also reduces the visual weight of the space.

BASIC BLACK

Black is not a color commonly used anywhere in domestic interiors, let alone the kitchen, but if your personal taste leans toward the dramatic it can be used to create a big impact. With its black laminate cabinetry, particleboard floor, deep stainless steel counters and an eye-catching stainless steel backsplash, this kitchen has a tough edge that aligns it with the industrial look. All three materials were delivered in sheet form and therefore required minimal installation time compared with labor-intensive alternatives, such as a tiled-and-grouted backsplash or a tongue-and-groove wooden floor. Innovative application of inexpensive materials, such as laminate and particleboard, also meant that a large part of the budget could be dedicated to the purchase of top-quality appliances.

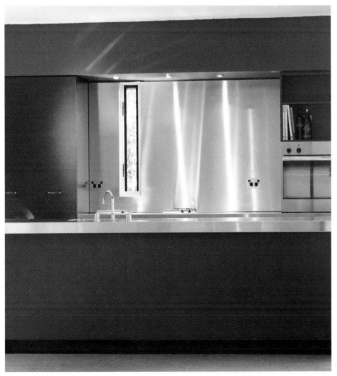

❶ The island functions as a food-preparation area for the kitchen, and as a servery for the adjacent dining room.

❷ Black laminate and stainless steel deliver a modern, sharp look, but are also extremely practical in a kitchen that sees plenty of cooking activity. The stainless steel is virtually invulnerable, immune to moisture, stains and heat, while the black laminate hides the splashes and splodges of a meal in progress.

❸ A louvered slit window behind the cooktop aids ventilation.

PLAY IT AS IT LAYS

Often kitchens are designed to downplay their functional nature, with dishwashers, refrigerators and microwave ovens concealed behind doors that match the surrounding cabinetry, but an industrial-style kitchen emphasizes its operational capacity, making a show of solid, hardworking appliances. A long terrazzo-topped island incorporating a massive range with double oven, extended cooktop and a ceiling-hung rangehood is the focus of this space. Task lighting likewise serves both as practical inclusion and chic design feature, with a set of downlights suspended on steel wires from the steeply pitched ceiling and additional spotlights mounted on long arms from the wall. A very pale stone paint color was chosen as a bridge between the warm tone of the wooden floor and the cool steel of the appliances.

❶ This massive island is a hardworking unit, incorporating an enormous range, a dishwasher and two sinks as well as drawers and surfaces for food preparation. The depth of the countertop makes it possible for cooks to work on one side while onlookers mill on the other. The second, outward-facing sink facilitates that, ensuring that cooks aren't obstructed by people needing a glass of water.

❷ Pendant lights hang low over the table, creating an intimate zone suitable for dining within a deliciously expansive space.

❸ Louvered windows and wooden shutters contribute to the engagingly loose structure and casual feel of this new kitchen. They also keep the space well ventilated.

SHOW YOUR METTLE

Apartments in converted industrial buildings tend to have open-plan arrangements. The absence of solid walls means owners can make the most of the lofty proportions and over-sized features of these industrial spaces. At the same time, domestic living requires a certain amount of containment to achieve a comfortingly human scale. The kitchen in this ex-factory apartment consolidates these two notions. A blade wall defines the space, screening the messy work of the kitchen from anyone entering through the front door. The wall stops short of the ceiling, leaving the area with its exposed pipes visibly intact. There is no fourth wall to the kitchen, so an agreeably open-plan look is maintained. The materials used in the fit-out are proudly utilitarian in character.

❶ The stainless steel counter-top sports an integrated sink, a shallow draining board and a wooden inset cutting surface.

❷ Much of the original character of the factory has been retained, with brick walls, structural supports and pipes left exposed.

❸ A partitioning wall defines the kitchen space and screens it off from the front door and entry hall.

① Opulent furnishings would have been obliterated by the rough, tough aesthetic of this refurbished factory. A simple, purposeful setting of trestle table and folding chairs, however, holds its own.

② These distinctive, super-sized windows are an asset to the apartment, acting as a generous source of natural light and contributing to the space's pared-back personality. They do, however, present a problem by prohibiting the installation of wall-hung cabinets. Metal-framed glass shelves provide the solution, delivering much-needed storage space without obstructing the light or inhibiting the character of the windows.

❶

❶ Two metal slide-out racks are fitted below the work surface, providing a handy storage spot for frequently used items. A guard rail ensures that stored items don't easily fall forward or backward when the rack is moved.

❷ The stainless steel counter running along the exterior wall is a permanent fixture, but all of the other units have been designed as free-standing pieces. Along the back wall, one steel-framed unit contains the oven and storage for appliances and pots. Next to it is a cabinet fronted with wire mesh. On the far right is a unit that conceals a refrigerator behind laminated door panels. These could easily be reconfigured within this kitchen or even be transported to an entirely new location.

❶

❶ Steel, glass and terrazzo — all trademark materials of the industrial look — are given a more graceful aspect in this kitchen. The tiled backsplash has a delicacy unknown to sheetform toughened glass. The door hardware, too, is particularly dainty.

❷ An overhang makes room for stools at a practical distance from the island's sink.

❷

LIGHT INDUSTRIAL

An industrial-style kitchen sits naturally in a city apartment building or a warehouse conversion, but it can also be tempered to suit a traditional family home. Terrazzo work surfaces, walls clad in stainless steel and large overhanging lightshades establish the industrial look in this kitchen, but are offset by more conservative elements, such as the simple and classic wooden cabinetry. The glass tiles of the backsplash bridge the gap, incorporating the look's trademark toughened glass, but in a tiled format that is more in keeping with a conventional family kitchen. An unusually long island with a sink and lever-handled faucets recalls the shape and style of school laboratories, yet avoids a clinical character thanks to the elegant doors of the cabinetry below.

❸ A conglomerate material made by setting stone chips in a concrete base, terrazzo was once a common sight in municipal buildings, but today is more likely to be seen in a sophisticated domestic setting. Modern terrazzo often features a tinted concrete base and more decorative aggregates, including colored glass or shell fragments, as seen in this countertop. ❸

BACK TO BASICS

The revival in suburban living has seen many style-conscious home owners moving into mass-produced old row houses and workers' cottages: rudimentary structures built to meet basic shelter needs, not designed to impress with decorative flourishes. Luxurious contemporary additions often sit awkwardly with the spartan character of these houses, and yet the very modern style of the industrial kitchen can work surprisingly well in the context. The industrial kitchen also focuses on the functional nature of a space, using hardy materials, such as concrete and steel, in their simplest forms. This kitchen is a case in point, its strong, purposeful aesthetic proving compatible with the unembellished nature of the original cottage. At the same time, it delivers a look and a structure worlds apart from the characteristically dark, cramped, inward-looking rooms of 19th-century architecture. Here, an open floorplan, walls of glazing and expansive doors that link indoor and outdoor spaces deliver a space for 21st-century lifestyles.

In an effort to subdue the visual impact of the kitchen in this open-plan environment, the owners requested that it present itself as a collection of free-standing pieces of furniture. Stony gray laminated cabinetry with integrated refrigerator, teamed with stainless steel counters, appliances and backsplash, functions as a monochrome backdrop in front of which stand the custom-made island and the dining table and chairs.

① The 12-foot (3.5-m) high ceilings match the proportions of the original part of the house, though they are treated in a very contemporary way. Almost all of the available vertical space is given over to glazing in a mixture of sliding windows, louvered windows and fixed glass panels. Wood-framed folding doors can be fully retracted, linking the furnished interior spaces with the wide and welcoming exterior deck.

② River stones were added to the concrete mix used for the countertop, resulting in a varied, slightly textured surface.

③ The island functions primarily as a food-preparation area for the kitchen, but it is also used as a breakfast bar, its generously proportioned surface easily accommodating a large unfolded newspaper. The massive weight of the island's concrete countertop necessitated the reinforcement of the floor.

4

FAMILY KITCHENS

From milk and cookies to Christmas dinners, the family
kitchen must be equipped to handle meals large or small,
simple or sophisticated, for one toddler or an entire dynasty.
It should also offer a warm welcome to all comers at all hours.
Opt for the practical over the precious, the friendly over the
finicky, the relaxed over the refined — and enjoy the results.

KEEPING IN THE LOOP

As well as being a practical room, a family kitchen ought to be the kind of place that draws people together and encourages them to enjoy each other's company. Although this kitchen has high creative values, with a curvaceous island that has the impact of a piece of sculpture, its greatest achievement is its hospitable interweaving of functional and recreational space. The loops of the counter create little islands where people can gather to work, sit, stand, eat or drink. Padded benches line the walls in a sunken corner of the space, forming a compact family room. In winter, the open fire draws a crowd, while in summer, wide folding windows and doors encourage a flow of traffic between the open-plan kitchen and the adjacent deck.

❶

❷

PREVIOUS PAGES A strip of copper faces the step down from the kitchen area into the family room. The inset light fixtures make it possible to move safely between the two spaces on cozy winter nights, when the overhead lights are turned off and the only source of illumination is the open fire.

❶ Shades of grape and chartreuse are strong enough to partner the dark tones of the jarrah hardwood cabinetry.

❷ Grape-colored panels and panels of jarrah veneer, including some that accommodate display niches, combine in a rhythmic pattern on the island's facade. That graphic rhythm is picked up by the grape-framed storage and display niches artfully deployed on the chartreuse back wall.

❸ Despite its eccentric character, this kitchen sacrifices nothing in terms of practicality. The need for storage space is amply served, albeit in visually stimulating ways. For example, a long, thin purple column of wine storage has a capacity for more than two dozen bottles.

❸

FARM FRESH

Housed inside a converted barn, this kitchen has an unpretentious air and indestructible finishes just perfect for a lively family. Structural wooden beams have been left exposed throughout the space, their existing positions defining new features such as the expansive glazing above the main work surface. The rough, raw, unabashedly functional elements are matched by super-practical surfaces, including the stainless steel countertops and the laminated cabinetry. Carrara marble countertops and backsplashes have a softening effect, yet their stony good looks maintain a link with the barn's earthy style. A dining table, used by the family for casual meals, occupies one end of the kitchen. It's serviced by a second sink so that family members aren't obliged to access the main sink for something as simple as a glass of water. The rinsing sink's location close to doors that open onto the yard also makes it a handy spot to wash grubby hands before a meal.

❶ This converted barn is awash with natural light, creating a delightful, sunlit environment. The spaces between the structural beams have been glazed, a practical consideration that also ensures the rough-edged character of the interior is preserved. At the far end, barn doors were replaced by glazed industrial sliding doors.

❶

❷ By day, the barn's rambling proportions are a pleasure, but at night a little definition helps to give the space a comforting sense of enclosure. In the breakfast nook, a pool of light from a colored glass shade hung low over the table creates an intimate pocket for cozy family meals. ❷

SIMPLE SOLUTIONS

❶

❶ The overhanging countertop of the peninsula leaves
room for stools, creating a casual eating area in the kitchen.
The circular sink makes it possible for family members to get
a drink without entering the main body of the kitchen.

❷ A significant proportion of the budget for this kitchen
was spent on basic construction. Elements such as the
comprehensive lighting system, the counter-height awning
windows that aid ventilation and the sound system with
wall-mounted speakers may not have a decorative impact,
but they go a long way toward making the kitchen a
comfortable and inviting space for a young family.

① A blade wall of steel-framed glass and wood forms a shallow foyer just inside the front door. The partition acts as a buffer between the entrance and the free-flowing living, kitchen and dining areas inside.

The pressures of a growing family made it necessary for the owners of this house to build a new open-plan living area, encompassing living and dining areas and a centrally located kitchen. As is often the case with new building projects, the majority of the budget was spent simply on providing the architectural shell and the necessary plumbing and electrical work. Consequently, the kitchen had to be completed within very strict financial parameters. The key was simplicity. All of the cabinetry is birch topped with a hardy concrete counter-top. The appliances have been left exposed, saving on the cost of integrating panels. Wall-mounted cabinets, unremarkable in themselves, become the kitchen's most distinctive feature thanks to their unusual placement across a wall of glazing. A garden view, visible through that wall of windows, brings color, pattern and movement to an otherwise restrained space.

② A panel of switches controlling lights throughout the entire living area is located at the end of the peninsula.

③ A gap in the overhead cabinetry offers a garden view to anyone working at the sink and gives a pleasantly asymmetrical pattern to the kitchen.

MODERN MANNERS

Traditional kitchens are not the only choice in a period home. Approached with confidence, an unabashedly contemporary look can add energy and excitement to an otherwise low-key space, and avoids the air of insincerity that sometimes hangs around a reproduction kitchen. Colorful cabinets of lime and plum make a claim for modernity, establishing the design intentions of the space from the outset. While an authentic period kitchen could be limited in its use of fixtures, this space benefits from efficient storage space provided by masses of purpose-designed cabinetry. A flood of natural light from glazed panels in the ceiling and a delightful indoor-outdoor ambiance, facilitated by walls of retractable glass doors, make this kitchen a fresh and friendly space that naturally draws the family to gather in it.

❶ The flat roof of the kitchen extension contains clear glass panels, which illuminate the space by day. At night, light fixtures attached to the surface of the roof make a feature of the wood-paneled exterior of the original part of the house.

❶

❷ | ❸
—— | ——
❹ | ❺

❷ Skylights mark the point where the old room finishes and the new, flat-roofed addition begins. Along one wall, cabinets run floor to ceiling and wall to wall. Their uniformity helps to downplay their presence, yet they contain masses of storage space and a built-in laundry room.

❸ An antique clock is a wry inclusion. Hung right at the spot where the extension begins, it is a playful reminder of the vintage of the original house.

❹ The thick wooden beams used for the shelves connect visually with the wooden feature strip set below the work surfaces.

❺ Small appliances are stashed behind folding doors at the end of the countertop.

HAPPILY SEPARATED

Busy and conflicting schedules mean meals together have given way to single servings in many households. Typically, family kitchens are used by more than one cook at a time, making a floorplan that incorporates multiple workstations more appropriate than one that features a single work zone. Here, the kitchen is broken down into a number of different sections. The main work area is located on the back wall, where a run of cabinetry houses the major appliances and a pantry. On the left-hand wall, a shorter cabinet encompasses an appliance garage and a rinsing sink, making it a self-sufficient space for the preparation of light meals. A circular breakfast bar supplies the space with a casual eating area, while a raised bar on the back of the island serves as a screen for the work surfaces around the main sink, where dirty dishes often gather.

When colors that lie directly opposite on the color wheel are combined, the result is a striking and dynamic partnership. For that reason, woods with a yellow to orange tone often benefit from being teamed with a strong blue.

❶ The rear wall is where the serious business of cooking takes place. It's fitted with a cooktop, a double-door refrigerator, a microwave oven and a double oven. Adjacent to it, a run of cabinetry incorporates a sink and a storage cabinet, which contains all the facilities for making coffee.

❷ Positioning the cooktop slightly to one side of the available space, rather than centering it, leaves a decent amount of work surface on the left. The asymmetrical structure is disguised by the artful backsplash: a wavy-edged diagonal of stainless steel.

❸ The circular eating area is some distance away from the busiest areas of the kitchen. Its physical separation, reinforced by its unusual shape, gives it an identity independent of the kitchen. As a result, those sitting down for a cup of coffee or a light snack aren't made to feel that they are stationed in the middle of a working kitchen.

❶

② ③

FIT AND READY

Like many busy, modern families, the owners of this small home needed to design a space that would serve as kitchen, dining room, informal breakfast bar and home office, all in one. Fitted cabinetry provided the solution, meeting all the functional requirements of the space, while ensuring a consistent look and style throughout. A U-shaped formation of cabinets defines the working kitchen, although it contains only the cooktop, a dishwasher, the sink and limited storage space. The oven, microwave oven, refrigerator and pull-out pantry are housed in a bank of cabinetry on the opposite wall, which also incorporates desk space for a compact home office at the far end. By necessity, the oven has been left exposed, but the microwave oven and refrigerator are concealed behind cupboard doors.

❶ A subtle but varied palette gives this room its dynamic. The materials occupy a fairly restrained span of color, from the ice white and jade green of the cabinetry to the steel of appliances, door hardware and door frames. Beech veneer surfaces provide a contrast, but not a clash.

❶

❷ If a flat ceiling had been installed below the visible roof beams, the kitchen would have been very cramped indeed. As it is, the pitched ceiling gives this room some breathing space. The neutral tones of the walls and the tiled floor, and the fine lines of the track lighting suspended over the main work surface, also promote a feeling of spaciousness. ❷

CARTOON CORNER

Rather than battle the colorful chaos that is an inevitable part of life with young children, the owners of this kitchen opted to embrace it. The cartoon-like shades and shapes of the space create a vibrant backdrop, where a little bit of disorder doesn't look out of place. Stainless steel countertops — hardwearing, easy to clean and super-hygienic — are matched by the sparkle of anodized aluminum-laminated cabinetry in pumpkin, turquoise, silver and purple. The colors are thrown into focus by areas of jet-black cabinetry, and the smooth surface makes it easy to wipe up the spills and smudges of a family kitchen. Slatted wooden screens are an innovative alternative to solid walls. They maintain sightlines with the adjacent living space and ensure a free flow of light and air around the house, yet they form a visual barrier between the kitchen and the neighboring living area, where the palette is more conservative. The screens can also be pulled across to form an interlocking wall when a more defined separation is required.

❶ A refrigerator, pantry and storage cabinet for small appliances are ranged down one side of the main body of the kitchen. A long stainless steel counter with sinks at either end occupies the opposite wall.

❷ In the narrow wing of what is essentially an L-shaped kitchen, a curving wooden breakfast bar forms a boundary with the adjacent family room.

❸ A panel of textured glass occupies an unusual void between the top of the back-splash and the bottom edge of a blade wall, which supports the hood. The open construction means that light from the stairwell window reaches the kitchen.

FREE-RANGING STYLE

❶

❶ The solid unit at the end of the island serves many purposes: it gives definition to the kitchen space, it screens the work surfaces from the dining area, and it provides a handy storage place for small appliances.

❷ The kitchen is the vantage point from which children can be seen playing either inside or outside the house. It's the structure of the space that makes it so well suited to family use, but its sense of style comes from the urbane pairing of pale blond maple and jet-black granite.

Open-plan living areas are an ideal environment for families with young children, allowing the little ones to have their free-running independence while parents supervise from a distance, getting on with their own work at the same time. If there's a common flaw among open-plan kitchens, though, it's that in the absence of solid walls they can be left to float, looking like a design afterthought in an otherwise cohesive house, and leaving cooks — and their chaos — exposed. The key to this open-plan kitchen is the narrow strip of cabinetry at the end of what is essentially an island. The cabinetry runs from floor to ceiling, forming a dividing wall between the kitchen and the adjacent dining room. Narrow enough to maintain sightlines throughout the space, it nonetheless anchors the kitchen, defining its dimensions and providing some cover for messy work surfaces.

❶ Like many open-plan kitchens, this space gives the impression of being larger than it is. In fact, it is essentially a modest two-wall galley construction. One wall houses the refrigerator, range and pantry. The pantry and a cupboard above the refrigerator were given a gray finish to balance the pale wooden cabinetry and dark countertops.

❷ Rather than a conventional high-gloss polish, the granite was given a honed finish. The low sheen is consistent with the kitchen's understated style.

❸ The island incorporates a double sink, a dishwasher and sliding storage shelves.

❶ ❶ The flow of cross breezes is facilitated by floor-to-ceiling louvered windows and by the counter-height awning window that opens onto a courtyard. The room takes a streamlined approach to design. Ample storage below the work surfaces is augmented by a walk-in pantry at the end of the kitchen. The island is also faced with cabinets on the dining room side. These have push-open operation, eliminating the need for door hardware and thus presenting an almost seamless facade.

❷

❷ All of the storage in the main body of the kitchen is provided by drawers, rather than cabinets. The designer and the owners agreed that these had greater space efficiency and were more comfortable to use.

A FRESH START

Much has been made of the need for the appliances and preparation surfaces in a kitchen to form an efficient work triangle, but this assumes that only one cook is working at any given time. Increasingly, though, the kitchen is the venue for more hybrid activity, with many cooks contributing to the preparation of one meal or with teenagers drifting in and out and catering to their own needs. This kitchen was designed with two distinct workstations, both of which have easy access to the refrigerator. One is centered around the cooktop, where deep drawers house pots and pans, and utensils hang from a wall-mounted rail. The other is the island, which incorporates the sink and dishwasher, purpose-built storage for glasses and plenty of counter space for food preparation. The open-plan construction links the kitchen with the surrounding living areas. A counter-height awning window on the exterior wall connects the space to an outdoor dining area. When the window is open, the counter services both the internal and external spaces.

5

SMALL KITCHENS

Lack of space is no excuse for poor kitchen design. The floorplan of a small kitchen — like one for a kitchen of any size — should address the fundamentals: storage capacity, light quality and safe and efficient work zones. Of course, size restrictions make the fulfillment of these basic requirements that little bit harder. Just set your priorities, succumb to logic and the rest will follow.

PERFECTLY FORMED

Apartment kitchens pose particular problems for the refurbisher. Rarely is it possible to remove walls, install windows or shift plumbing, so a kitchen refit usually necessitates working within some very tight constraints. This kitchen refurbishment overcomes space restrictions by wrapping fitted cabinetry around from the kitchen walls into the hallway, thus eking out some extra storage room and visually increasing the size of the space. White marble countertops and backsplashes, sandblasted glass doors on overhanging cabinetry and an ivory color scheme make the most of what little natural light is available. They also conform to the gentle palette used throughout the apartment.

PREVIOUS PAGES Maintaining a monochrome palette and opting to integrate appliances reduces visual disruptions in a confined space. The porcelain sink was placed at right angles to the wall, an unorthodox orientation that makes full use of the depth of the counter while taking up as little as possible of the horizontal stretch of work surfaces. Open shelving above the sink allows an element of personality to penetrate the space's otherwise very restrained, composed countenance.

❶ All cabinets are fitted with sliding shelves, ensuring that every last bit of storage space is fully utilized. A protruding wall at the far end of the room is camouflaged by marble facing and a bank of wall units styled and sized to match those nearer the entrance.

ALONE TOGETHER

Rather than surrender the total floor area to a U-shape format, this artful kitchen designed for an urban couple is contained within a protruding peninsula. This provides maximum work space and allows the living area to extend alongside the kitchen. The broad, stainless steel countertop is positioned so that it can be accessed from either side, making the most of its facility as a work surface. It also incorporates a small cooktop at the outer end and a double sink supplemented with a draining bowl for fresh herbs and salad leaves at the end closest to the wall. A half-size dishwasher is located at counter height adjacent to those sinks, forming a tight work zone for cleaning activities. A simple window seat furnishes the space with a sitting area that can be used by kitchen spectators while the cook is preparing the meal.

❶ A section of open storage is an advantage in even the smallest of kitchens. It makes frequently used items blissfully easy to access and it presents an opportunity to showcase the household's personality through its choice of tableware and collectibles.

❶

❷ Small spaces benefit from fuss-free finishes, but that doesn't mean they have to be characterless. The recessed door handles and drawer pulls of this cabinetry ensure a seamless facade, but the soft yellow tone of the laminate imbues the space with character. ❷

DISPLAY CASE

A desire for increased living spaces led to a drastic reduction in floor size for this kitchen, which is part of an open-plan refurbishment. A wall between the old kitchen and dining room was removed and replaced with a counter that defines the new boundary, with a larger dining space and a shortened kitchen. The counter is suspended between two upright partitions, which conceal some of the space's messier areas. Behind one is a series of open shelves, which store cookbooks and small appliances. The other serves as a backsplash for a cooktop and provides a wall for the installation of a hood. Stainless steel counters and metallic surfaces on the cabinetry complement the stainless steel appliances, forming a mono-chromatic scheme that is the perfect backdrop for the owners' dramatic art collection.

❶

❷

❶ A stainless steel refrigerator, steel dishwasher drawers and a steel oven blend seamlessly with surrounding steel counters and metallic-finish cabinets. The simplified palette of the kitchen was designed to complement these high-quality appliances in a timeless and classic way, guaranteeing that the look doesn't age before they do.

❷ A brushed finish to the stainless steel counters will camouflage most of the inevitable fingerprints and scratch marks.

❸ Extensive floor-to-ceiling cabinetry around the appliances on the rear wall ensures that the kitchen loses none of its storage capacity despite the drop in floor size.

❸

SMALL PACKAGES

Storage is a key issue in small kitchens. Having removed a wall between the kitchen and the neighboring dining room to bring light and openness to their house, the owners then installed in its place a bank of cabinetry to give the different zones some definition and provide storage space for both rooms. On the dining side, drawers with recessed aluminum strip pulls house telephone books and a pull-out ironing board. A built-in window seat also conceals storage space. In the kitchen, a rear wall of cabinetry houses an integrated refrigerator and two pantry cabinets. Both end units extend to the ceiling, providing a place to keep infrequently used items and giving the kitchen a theatrical and symmetrical backdrop.

The counter that forms a boundary with the adjacent living area provides a long stretch of work surface, while the back wall of the kitchen is given over to the oven, cooktop, integrated refrigerator and a concentrated supply of storage space. Plywood cabinetry is a stylistic link to the wooden paneling characteristic of the original interior finishes of the early 20th-century house. Recessed aluminum drawer pulls and door handles give the space a contemporary detail and have proved satisfyingly childproof — an unexpected bonus for the young parents.

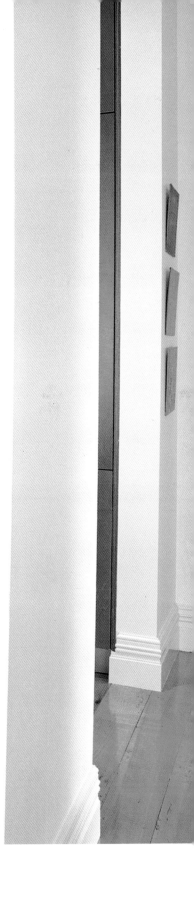

①

THE LADDER OF SUCCESS

The surest way of achieving success in a small space is to keep it simple, keep it light and keep it white. Here, all three of those tactics were employed in installing not only a kitchen but also a living and dining area, a laundry room and a study in an extremely tight space. A galley floorplan in the kitchen provides maximum spatial efficiency, keeping all the appliances and work surfaces within a few steps of each other. The peninsula countertop is accessible from the living area so that one cook can stand outside the kitchen area while another is inside at the range. Plenty of daylight and a plain white approach to walls and cabinets keep the whole area looking as spacious as possible.

① Small-space design means making the most of whatever is available. Here, a neat floorplan makes space for living and dining areas as well as a laundry room and a kitchen, plus a mezzanine-level room accessed by a ladder and used as a spare bedroom. Expert engineering allows the room to be suspended from the ceiling, eliminating the need for supporting pillars that would have intruded on floorspace at ground level.

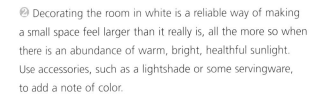

❷ Decorating the room in white is a reliable way of making a small space feel larger than it really is, all the more so when there is an abundance of warm, bright, healthful sunlight. Use accessories, such as a lightshade or some servingware, to add a note of color.

❸ A section of the available space was closed off to satisfy the owners' request for a separate laundry room. The extra-broad granite countertop runs down the outside of the internal wall to form a simple desk.

❹ Small dimensions can be used to advantage in a work space such as the kitchen. Here, the range, the sink, a full-height pantry and the refrigerator are just a few steps away from one another. Despite the compactness of the fitout, the floorplan allows for extensive counter space either side of the sink.

①

CATCHING THE BUZZ

A Japanese-inspired kitchen design might not be the obvious choice for a 19th-century cottage, but where better to turn for small space solutions than the crowded metropolis of Tokyo? To save on building costs, a decision was made to retain the split floor level of the old kitchen. A U-shaped work area was installed on the upper portion and a petite dining setting on the lower level. Storage runs all the way to the ceiling and incorporates numerous areas of open shelving. In particular, open storage of cooking ingredients and pots and pans avoids the need for frequent opening and closing of drawers and cabinets, an activity that can lead to much congestion in a small kitchen. The multiplicity of surface materials is an unusual ploy, providing a variety of stimuli that distracts the eye from the room's awkward dimensions.

① Interior walls are stacked with storage, but exterior walls are given over to glazing so that the room receives as much light as possible.

②

② A checkered glass wall lines the corridor at an angle, a deliberate device to give the impression of a fast-receding Tokyo alleyway.

③ Dark colors and busy lines are commonly avoided in small spaces, but here they quite deliberately recreate the buzzy commotion of Asian street markets.

③

COOKS' KITCHENS

To the passionate cook, a kitchen is more than a work space.
It's a studio, a source of inspiration, a place to linger over
well-thumbed cookbooks and a treasury of hand-me-down
family recipes. Naturally it ought to have a sensible floorplan
and a collection of high-performance appliances, but it must
also be a pleasure to inhabit.

CORE BUSINESS

Cooking enthusiasts dream of having a roomy space in which to work, and yet, without careful planning, a large kitchen can be terribly inefficient. With that in mind, this very spacious kitchen was designed with a tight work zone at its center, formed by the impressive range and two islands. The range, which has two hot plates and four ovens that bake at different temperatures, is without doubt the working showpiece of the kitchen. The two nearby islands provide long and broad granite countertops for food preparation and are fitted with refrigerator drawers, freezer drawers, a dishwasher, a rinsing sink and power outlets for small appliances. Beyond this central core, counters provide space for serving and presenting food, and for cleaning tasks.

PREVIOUS PAGES Housed in one of the kitchen's peripheral islands, this functional range is a serious cook's dream. Four different ovens work at four different temperatures to deliver very precise results. Behind the island, a casual table setting occupies a sunlit location next to the glazed wall.

❶ The kitchen's lighting requirements are met by skylights, tracklights that provide task lighting and pendant and ceiling-mounted fixtures for ambient lighting.

❷ A second oven, an additional hotplate and a microwave oven are located on the back wall. Such an array of appliances makes it possible for many cooks to work at once — or for one cook to prepare a variety of foods using many different methods.

❸ This well-equipped space also contains a television, which is visible from the food-preparation areas.

① An integrated ventilation unit is located under the raised servery, visible immediately behind the range. The alternative would have been an overhead hood, but installation would have been difficult due to the room's cathedral ceilings and the range's location in a freestanding island.

② This spacious kitchen incorporates several work zones. The central zone is defined by the range and the two islands running perpendicular to it, one of which incorporates refrigerator drawers while the other features a sink and a dishwasher. Another zone is created along an outer wall where storage for glassware, a refrigerator and a half-width dishwasher are gathered together to form a bar area.

THREE-PART HARMONY

❶

❶ Laminated cabinetry the color of coffee grounds, teak end panels, white laminate countertops and stainless steel strip edging combine in a palette with a fashion edge. The combination is neutral enough to survive the decorative shifts of time with just a change of accessories.

❷ The multiple accessories that come with this sink keep the surrounding work surfaces as free from clutter as possible, an important consideration in a small kitchen.

❷

A thriving cook's kitchen doesn't have to be a rambling room with a great abundance of space. Provided that the storage space is well organized and the work areas are thoughtfully designed, it can be as petite as this little kitchen, which measures barely 100 square feet (10 sq m). Despite those space restrictions, the kitchen features three work zones. The first is the cooking zone, with an extra-large cooktop and oven set into a wall of cabinetry and a storage rack providing ready access to utensils and spices. The second is the food-preparation zone, which incorporates a super-sized sink and a counter broad enough to accommodate seated guests. A wall of tall cabinets makes up the third zone, providing storage for tableware, cookbooks and food items.

❶ The pantry's stainless steel fittings optimize the available space. The central pull-out core of swinging shelves ensures that every single item can be reached easily and that none of the interior is wasted. Unsurprisingly, units like these come at a high price, but super-efficient storage is a priority in a small kitchen and funds must be allocated to its provision.

❶

❷ The back wall of the kitchen is intensively fitted out. The commercial-grade oven is flanked to the left by deep drawers for pot storage and on the right by a mini pull-out pantry stocked with cooking condiments. A rail runs the length of the wall, supporting more oils, spices and preserves, and essential cooking utensils.

❷

❶ Rather than install another solid facade, the designer opted to front the pantry with etched glass doors. It's a strategy that provides some visual breathing space in an intensively equipped kitchen.

❷ The kitchen's elaborately accessorized rail storage system offers a book holder to the left of the cooktop and racks for paper towels and plastic film to the right.

❷

RETRO-VISION

Highly efficient work spaces don't have to have the severe aesthetic of a commercial kitchen. As this colorful kitchen shows, they can be bright and friendly and even sport something of a retro feel. The butterfly-wing formation of the cabinetry harks back to the kidney-shaped curves of the 1950s, but also supplies the kitchen with its most innovative feature: a work zone structured so that the cooktop, food-preparation area and sink can be reached with just a swinging action by the cook. This structure also provides extra countertop space without crowding the kitchen as much as a freestanding island would in the same area. The yellow of the cabinetry is the element that gives the kitchen its personality — and yet it costs no more than a more conservative color choice.

❸ A bulkhead in a yellow finish to match the cabinetry extends over the work area. It brings the height of the downlights closer to the countertops so that they can deliver stronger, surer illumination. Bulkheads are also a useful way of installing downlights in rooms where the ceiling cannot be tampered with, for example in an apartment kitchen. **❸**

CLINICAL PRECISION

Practical considerations, such as creating a low-maintenance, ultra-hygienic kitchen for a large family, don't have to mean a sacrifice of style, as this kitchen shows. Countertops of stainless steel and marble meet the owners' requirements for hardwearing, easy-to-clean work surfaces, while providing a sophisticated contrast with the deep burgundy, lacquered wooden cabinetry. Behind the elegant facade of etched glass doors, the extensive pantry offers plenty of storage space for the family of seven. Even the eye-catching, wall-mounted spice rack manages to be both fashionable and functional, keeping the cook's condiments close to hand while freeing up countertop and cabinet space.

❶ Spending money on elements that lie beneath the surface can be difficult when more instantly gratifying features beckon. After a few months or years of constant use, however, you will be glad of a drawer that glides shut without banging or sticking.

❶

❷ Downlights in the ceiling provide general illumination while task lighting is delivered by recessed lights in overhanging bulkheads and striplights on the underside of wall cabinets.

❸ Etched glass doors make a design feature of the pantry. The cabinet usually comes with glass shelves, but the fastidious owners requested stainless steel for extra strength.

❹ The showstopping feature of the kitchen is its brilliant red cabinetry. The color is used sparingly and in distinct blocks so as not to overwhelm the space.

❺ A utility sink is located in the island, close to the cooktop. The main sink, set against a wall, is used for washing dishes, but this one is reserved for tasks relating to food preparation.

At Home with the Cook

Focusing too much on supplying super-durable surfaces and super-performance fittings in an effort to create the ultimate cook's kitchen can result in a room that functions brilliantly, but fails to be an asset to the house. Here, commercial-grade appliances and a stainless steel work surface were softened by the use of handsome cherry-wood cabinetry, custom made to suit the home's 1940s vintage. A pale gray granite was sourced and used on surfaces surrounding the cooktop, a gentler look than that of the more common black granite and a subtle companion to the stainless steel used elsewhere. These carefully selected finishes give the space a warm and homey character without compromising its efficiency or its quality.

An authentic 1940s kitchen would have had none of the features that make this space so desirable to the enthusiastic home cook: the efficient planning, high-quality appliances or generous proportions. Nonetheless, the wooden cabinetry with its hooded drawer pulls accurately evokes the vintage of the house. The result is a kitchen that doesn't immediately register as a "new" piece of work within a charming old house.

① Stainless steel countertops can be custom made to incorporate sinks. An integrated sink means fewer joins and edges to harbor grime, mildew and bacteria. A commercial restaurant supplier was contracted to fabricate this L-shaped counter.

② Particular attention has been paid to the design of the outer face of the island to make it an active zone rather than a passive facade. A curved granite countertop nestles in the elbow of the island. At the top end, shelves contain a library of cookbooks. The result is a comfortable, casual eating area, a sociable spot for kitchen spectators and a welcoming nook in which passionate cooks can indulge in some cookbook browsing.

③ Extensive glazing supplies the kitchen with abundant natural light during the day. The multi-paneled windows are designed to suit the character of the 1940s-era house, but also to enhance the garden outlook, the smaller panes echoing the lacy canopy of the trees. The upper casement windows can be wound open, encouraging cooking aromas to drift up and out of the kitchen.

WING TIPS

Small spaces always profit from innovative thinking, but the design of this compact apartment kitchen benefits from a most unusual approach to floorplan. Rather than a conventional U-shaped arrangement, the kitchen is fitted with cabinets that splay out in butterfly-wing formation. One "wing" contains the cooktop, the other the sink. Half-drum, swing-out drawers below waist level make the most of the curved space. On the cooktop wing they are used to house jars of spices and bottles of oils and sauces; on the sink wing they hold tableware and storage containers. The result of these innovative forms and fixtures is that the cook is almost surrounded by work surfaces, making the most of the very limited space available.

❶ Deep drawers to the right of the oven store pots and pans, while the slim drawer below it is used for flat baking trays.

❷ Sinks that feature removable, integrated cutting boards can extend the work surfaces in a kitchen with limited space.

❸ Some hoods are fitted with lights that fulfill the role of task lighting at the cooktop. It's a space-saving bonus, especially in an apartment setting, where ceiling installation poses structural and bureaucratic hassles.

CLASSIC KITCHENS

Nostalgic or ultra modern, warm and organic, or cool and steely, there's one quality that all classically styled kitchens have in common: timelessness. Whether the intention is to install a kitchen that looks as if it has been standing for a hundred years, or to create one that will stand up to scrutiny a hundred years hence, a classic kitchen will always be characterized by quiet authority.

ICE PRINCESS

All-white color schemes are something of a kitchen standard. Their simplicity and their air of cleanliness and calm appeal — but they can look a little too antiseptic and sometimes lack the sense of personality that makes a good kitchen great. Here, snow white and ice blue team up to offer all the cool, clean advantages of a pure-white kitchen, but without the anonymity that can come with a monochromatic palette. The blue is a stylish match for the stainless steel appliances as well as being a reference to the home's seaside location. All the blue surfaces are in fact backpainted glass, a design element that lends the space an exquisite luminosity.

PREVIOUS PAGES An abundance of space is always welcome in the kitchen, but unless cabinets are scaled to match the impressive dimensions, the room can end up looking awkward. In this kitchen, which measures almost 20 feet (7 m) wide, an island 12 feet (4.5 m) in length ensures a sense of spatial balance.

❶ Taking full advantage of the room's generous proportions, wall units were extended all the way to the ceiling, providing a large amount of storage space. While the floor-to-ceiling expanse of cabinetry works successfully in this roomy kitchen, it can be claustrophobic in a smaller space.

❶

❷ Backpainted glass has been used as a feature surface on components of the cabinetry less likely to be subjected to constant wear and tear. The cabinets and drawers in the main work area have a more durable lacquered finish. A matching backpainted backsplash and a door that leads to a walk-in pantry bring inserts of the color to the hardworking rear wall of the kitchen.

❷

A FINE BALANCE

Devising a hardworking, open-plan kitchen that has the refinement to match a classically styled home requires special effort. Here, aluminum edging on the counters and long, slim aluminum door handles give some fine lines to otherwise standard laminated cabinetry. A fixed base was required for the island in order to conceal the plumbing that runs to the rinsing sink. To avoid a heavy-set appearance, the base was set back and aluminum legs were used to support the outer edges of the cabinetry. This structure creates the impression that the island is a freestanding unit. A short overhang at one end of the island forms a casual eating area, furnished with two tall chairs, which contribute to the sophisticated look of the work space. The creamy tone of the cabinetry and the buttery shade of the walls also enhance the graceful ambiance of the space.

❶ A mellow paint color is influential in uniting the three zones of this long, narrow room. The delicate detailing of the kitchen cabinetry also plays a role in ensuring that the kitchen is compatible with the slightly formal living areas, with their fine-boned furniture pieces and soft-hued fabrics.

❶

❷ A slim cabinet fits between the range and the refrigerator and is used to store cooking oils and condiments. The pantry, with its aluminum-framed glass doors, was built over an existing window. The windowpanes were frosted to soften the exterior view.　❷

BEST DRESSED

In a tiny cottage, this area with less than 100 square feet (10 sq m) of floorspace had to accommodate not only all the trappings of a modern kitchen, but a dining table too. The solution was to arrange appliances and cabinetry along two walls of the room, making use of the available height by running the overhead cabinets all the way to the ceiling. A standard refrigerator would have overwhelmed the little room if left unconcealed, so it has been integrated into a unit made to look like a freestanding dresser. The stepped-back wings of the dresser-style cabinet give the piece elegant lines but are in fact a legacy of the space restrictions: without them the refrigerator door would not have been able to open fully and entry into the room would have been obstructed.

Cream-colored paneled cabinetry topped with a wooden molding gives this kitchen a mildly traditional look, appropriate for the vintage of the cottage in which it was installed. A stainless steel counter runs the length of one wall, introducing a smart, contemporary element that helps to make a connection between the modern appliances and the classic setting.

ALL IN THE DETAIL

By definition, classic kitchens should have a decorative subtlety that affords them a timeless quality, yet they need not be devoid of personality. The wood, granite and ceramic tiles that form the broad palette of this kitchen have universal appeal, but the details reveal the particular interests of the owners. The wooden inlays and hand-forged door handles and drawer pulls of the cabinetry are inspired by the early 20th-century work of Frank Lloyd Wright and give the kitchen a distinct character. Displayed in purpose-built cabinets, a collection of colorful ceramics puts a personal stamp on an otherwise elegantly low-key space.

❶ The aesthetic character of this kitchen cabinetry is achieved not by add-on decorative flourishes but by the inherent qualities of the natural materials. For example, strips of mahogany set into blond maple give the cabinet doors a handsome look.

② A central, structural column was required to turn three small rooms into one spacious open-plan area. The supporting column was designed as a pillar of cabinetry. On the kitchen side it contains a wall oven. On the opposite side, facing the living area, it houses a television. Surrounding these two appliances is a vast amount of storage space, including a purpose-built message center located directly in front of the internal garage door.

③ A moss-green, ceramic tile backsplash is in character with the early 20th-century design work that inspired this kitchen, and also makes a link with the display cases of collectible ceramics, which are a feature of the space.

④ The furniture of the dining setting displays fine craftsmanship in keeping with the detailed woodwork of the kitchen.

A DELICATE MATTER

With the last of their children having grown up and left home, the owners of this kitchen seized the opportunity to design a space that had all the refinement denied them during years of messy and demanding child raising. Their desire for a delicate-looking kitchen was made possible by a side wall of cabinetry housing a double-door refrigerator, an oven, a microwave oven, china storage, a pantry and even the air-conditioning unit. With those heavy-duty items out of the way, the balance of the kitchen could be furnished with petite parallel counters topped with granite and finished with wooden end panels, a design strategy employed to give the impression of freestanding pieces of furniture. Backpainted glass used on the backsplash and on the face of the island capitalizes on natural light coming in through newly installed french doors.

❷

❸

❶ No bulky appliances are visible in the area of the kitchen most exposed to the neighboring dining area. A cooktop installed in the granite countertop on the rear wall is scarcely discernible from a distance.

❷ Contrasting wooden end pieces give the peninsula a furnished look.

❸ The major appliances, including the house's air-conditioning unit, the refrigerator and the oven, are positioned together in elegant cabinetry on a side wall that is readily accessible from the main body of the kitchen but avoids exposure to the dining table.

ON THE FACE OF IT

Cabinetry with a traditional door profile was a natural choice in an open-plan living area that features a charming conservatory, classic parquetry flooring and a warm palette. The main work area of the U-shaped kitchen is defined by two walls of cabinetry and an island, all of them clad in practical off-white laminate. The laminate and the granite countertops present an appropriate environment for contemporary appliances that may have looked out of place in a less obviously functional setting. The wall that faces the living areas is lined with cabinetry faced in cherry wood rather than utilitarian laminate and is used primarily for the storage and display of tableware and servingware. The surface switch ensures that the kitchen presents a furnished face to the living and dining areas, downplaying its role as a work space.

Repetition of selected design features can give a large open-plan space a desirable sense of consistency. In this case, the distinctive, traditional detailing of the kitchen cabinetry is also apparent in the living area in an expanse of cabinetry that houses books and entertainment equipment.

① A wall of cherry-wood cabinetry is a feature of the kitchen, with glass-fronted cabinets showcasing a collection of ceramics. A double-door refrigerator is concealed behind solid wooden doors to one side of the display units.

② The decision to retain two original windows left little wall space on which to position a hood. The solution was to create a false wall against which the hood could sit, installing the cooktop across one corner of the kitchen.

DECEPTIVELY SIMPLE

The design of this elegant kitchen was approached from two perspectives. The first was a matter of structure. Located at the end of a long open-plan room, which also contains formal dining and living areas, this work space had to be as understated as possible, concealing or camouflaging all of the more utilitarian inclusions. Two elements in the floorplan of the galley kitchen achieve this aim. The first was the strategic positioning of the oven, cooktop and associated ventilation unit on a wall not readily visible from the dining area. The second was the installation of a walk-in pantry at the far end of the room. A glass-doored display case built into the cavity wall of the pantry draws the focus, cleverly disguising the presence of the storage room behind.

The other starting point was a desire to continue the sophisticated organic palette established elsewhere in the house. Here, a combination of oak cabinetry, marble counters and backsplashes, and metal fixtures is used to give the room a streamlined look imbued with a natural, textural warmth.

❶ A textured finish to the glass doors of the display case casts a veil over the contents. Instead of being fully exposed, the plates and drinking glasses are seen primarily as silhouettes. The emphasis on shape makes the most of everyday items of tableware that might not necessarily be showpieces.

❶

❷ Most of the storage space is concealed, but a small amount of open storage allows the kitchen to function efficiently. Clustered around the cooktop and oven, an extensive hanging-rail system and some shelves keep regularly used cooking tools, condiments and tableware close to hand. ❷

❶ The twin sinks were undermounted so that nothing would interfere with the counter's smooth sweep of marble. A light paint wash was applied to the oak cabinetry — not enough to obscure the grain, but just enough to temper the wood tone.

❶

❷ Brushed stainless steel toeboards are an obvious choice, given the use of metal elsewhere. The stainless steel is also a tonal match for the gracefully veined marble, achieving a delicate balance of color throughout the kitchen.

❷

GRAND DEMANDS

A residence of imposing proportions and magnificent surfaces, including thick walls of hand-quarried sandstone, demanded a brand-new kitchen that would match the sense of grandeur. Though the structure of the open-plan kitchen and its fixtures — including a multi-fuel cooktop and a water-filter tap — are plainly contemporary, the space has a timeless quality about it. All of the door and drawer fronts were painted in cream, detailed in blue, then treated to produce a weathered finish. The resulting surface is a comfortable companion for those warmly textured sandstone walls. Though the floor level drops, the ceiling height remains constant throughout the open-plan area, resulting in an unusually high ceiling in the kitchen. Tall wall cabinets take the total height of the cabinetry above the counter to an impressive 8 feet (2.5 m) — with another 2½ feet (75 cm) of exposed wall above that.

❶ The change in floor height between the kitchen and the living areas presented an opportunity for storage space. A bank of drawers and some custom-built wine storage fit neatly in the neighboring living area's subfloor cavity without consuming any of the kitchen's floorspace.

❶

❷ Working with a kitchen cabinet supplier to customize standard fixtures can enhance the look of a space without excessively increasing costs. In this case, standard units were used for base cabinets but extra-tall wall cabinets were specially built to match the scale of the room. All of the paneled door and drawer fronts were given a paint finish that suits the age-worn charms of the kitchen. ❷

OPEN FOR INSPECTION

In a house characterized by high design standards, this fairly small open-plan kitchen was charged with presenting a stylish face from all vantage points, including the nearby living and dining areas, several internal corridors and the luxurious lap pool. Although it had to provide plenty of storage space within a small floor area and function as the house's main kitchen, it was also expected to look more like a furnished room than a work space. The solution was a distinguished composition of surfaces with richly striped walnut veneer base units topped by a slick, ivory-toned counter. An integrated sink and dishwasher pose little disruption to the handsome, contrasting planes of color. Overhead cabinets provide a massive amount of storage capacity, but their presence scarcely registers, the finely framed glass door fronts blending into the background along with the painted glass backsplash.

❶ The presence of a stainless steel wall oven was impossible to disguise. As a compromise, it was positioned on a short side wall not readily visible from the living areas.

❶

❷ The marked difference between the intense hue and grain of the walnut veneer and the luminous surfaces of the glass door fronts and backsplash renders the fixtures above counter height all but invisible. This device serves to create an illusion of spaciousness in a room that is really quite small.

❷

TAKING CENTER STAGE

Part of the refurbishment of a house that accommodates a family of six, including four teenagers, this open-plan expanse was designed with the kitchen as its physical and social center-piece. The space is exposed to the formal and casual eating areas located at either end and to the living areas to the front. The kitchen is given definition by structural columns, which bracket the island, and a lowered ceiling, which facilitates the installation of recessed task lighting. The distance between the two parallel walls of the galley kitchen was made particularly broad so that all six family members could comfortably occupy the space at once. A freestanding wooden counter in the middle of the kitchen serves as a work surface for the cooktop, which is surrounded by hefty appliances and storage units.

The island that faces out toward the living areas and the garden space beyond is the kitchen's primary work surface. It also hides a dishwasher behind a panel of wood veneer.

❶ The kitchen's rear wall accommodates a double oven, microwave oven, cooktop, hood, refrigerator and full-height pantry, as well as some additional storage space. Aside from the elbow room necessary for safe and comfortable use of the cooktop, the appliance-heavy rear wall has almost no counter space. A freestanding wooden counter serves as a work surface, providing a handy resting place for cooking ingredients and saucepans.

❶

❷ The broad dimensions of the galley kitchen emphasize the free-flowing character of the space. Open shelving installed in the living area ensures that the kitchen's views throughout the interior and right out into the garden areas are unobstructed.

❷

8

PLANNING

The pleasure of reaching out and finding a pepper grinder just where it is needed, of completing a simple task in perfect light, of clearing the counters with ease or unloading the dishwasher without having to trek across the room or circumnavigate other members of the household: these are the enormously satisfying rewards of an efficient kitchen floorplan.

WORK ZONES

Other rooms in the house have their function, but the kitchen is primarily a work space. It is used at least twice a day, and certainly every day of the week. Under such constant pressure, any flaws in its design or any inefficiencies in its structure will soon make themselves ceaselessly and irritatingly apparent.

THE CLASSIC WORK TRIANGLE

The much-talked-about kitchen work triangle is a concept that originated in the 1950s, when both science and architecture were interested in the idea that floorplans could be used to create maximum efficiency in a home. It was founded on the notion that there must be an ideal spatial relationship between the three main activity centers — the cooktop, the refrigerator and the sink — that could be applied to a variety of kitchen shapes. The conclusion was that, in order for a cook to work easily and comfortably, the three legs of the triangle formed by those sites should add up to a total of 20 feet (7 m). Any more and the cook would have to trudge long distances between one activity and the next; any less and she would be too cramped.

PREVIOUS PAGES Traditionally, sinks were placed on one of the exterior walls, where plumbing was easy to access and a window could provide light and ventilation. More and more often in contemporary kitchens, sinks are located on islands or peninsulas that also serve as breakfast bars. Sinks in this position can be used by household members to pour a glass of water or fill the kettle without disrupting the work of the cook.

❶ In a galley kitchen, sink and cooktop can be placed near each other on parallel counters with plenty of work surface on either side.

Of course, the theoretical model is not always easily applied in the real-life kitchen, but the basic principle that the distance between these three points should be neither too great nor too small is sound. In essence, a work triangle should be proportioned so that the cook only needs to take a few steps between any of the three activity centers, and so that there is adequate elbow room at each of those sites. The triangle may span a galley kitchen, a U- or L- shaped kitchen or a kitchen that incorporates an island. When applied to a "one-wall" or "single-line" kitchen, the triangle flattens into a straight line, but the principles remain the same: just a few steps between the three main points and plenty of room to stand and work at each one.

If the shape of your kitchen necessitates a sprawling triangle, try at least to have the sink and the cooktop located at either end of one of the shorter legs, since it is between these two sites that you will often need to work quickly, carrying heavy, and usually hot, pots and pans. Ideally, the space between them should incorporate a reasonable run of clear counter space, as this tends to become the chief food-preparation zone: a step in one direction and you're at the sink for rinsing and washing, a step in the other and you're at the cooktop. Little will be lost in the way of efficiency by having the refrigerator positioned at some distance from these two — in fact it could increase efficiency, given that other family members often drift in and out of the kitchen grabbing drinks or snacks from the refrigerator and potentially getting under the feet of the cook. Try to avoid having the kitchen door located within the triangle: such a configuration will force household traffic to cross the cook's path, a source of irritation and potential danger for all involved.

❶ In this compact kitchen, the refrigerator is located beyond the work area, defined by parallel counters. It can be used by anyone looking to fetch a snack without trespassing on the cook's main activity zone, yet it is near enough to those sites for easy access.

❶

❷ A substantial stretch of counter space between the range and the sink serves as this kitchen's primary food-preparation area. The counter that extends as a peninsula to the right of the sink functions as an additional work surface as required, but more commonly does duty as a breakfast bar.

❷

❶

❶ A split-level island counter creates two functional zones in a single work area. The full-height counter is used for most food-preparation activities, while the lowered section is tailor-made for weight-bearing tasks, such as kneading and rolling.

❷ A classic kitchen presents a slight twist on the conventional work triangle. The three main work sites — refrigerator, sink and range — are located close to one another, but the sink is positioned on a peninsula in a style favored in contemporary kitchen design. The placement of the sink makes it easy for family members to clear dirty dishes from the dining table to the sink, where they can be rinsed and then stacked in the nearby dishwasher.

❷

① A peninsula with an unusual stainless steel plinth base divides this kitchen in two. One half of the kitchen contains the work area, with refrigerator, oven, microwave oven, cooktop and sinks. The other half features storage, but can also function as an additional area for food preparation.

② The small dimensions of this compact galley kitchen meant that work surfaces had to be prioritized. A decision was made to forgo counter space around the range in favor of storage. Counters around the sink serve as a food-preparation area and make room for serving meals and clearing plates.

WORKSTATIONS

In the 1950s, when the work triangle was devised, the kitchen was chiefly inhabited by only one person: the woman of the household. As wife, mother, cook and housekeeper, she was responsible for all meal preparation and all cleaning activities.

Social developments over the last half century have changed the way the kitchen is used and therefore have had an impact on the design of the modern kitchen. It remains true that a well-designed kitchen should be easy for a single cook to negotiate. It is also the case that multiple cooks can be involved in the preparation of a single meal, or that more than one meal is being prepared by more than one member of the household at a given time, or that other activities, such as children's homework, are taking place while meal preparation is in progress.

For that reason, the idea of designing kitchens with multiple workstations is taking hold. For example, locating the refrigerator and the microwave oven close together at some distance from the cooktop could provide a facility for teenagers to organize snacks for themselves and their friends even as another meal is being prepared. Installing an appliance garage, equipped with kettle, toaster and breakfast provisions, at the end of a breakfast bar with seating creates a self-sufficient breakfast spot. In a serious cook's kitchen, a second sink, used solely for food-preparation tasks and surrounded by a good amount of counter space, is a delightfully functional luxury. So, too, is a pastry-making counter, located close to the oven and set at a height of 30 inches (76 cm) rather than the standard 36 inches (92 cm) to provide an ergonomically sound surface for kneading and rolling. There is no one-size-fits-all formula to this more complex concept of kitchen design, as the number and the nature of the workstations are defined by the needs of the household.

① In a corner of the kitchen, a small snack-ready work zone is created by the installation of a microwave oven, an appliance garage faced with a roller door and the electrical outlets necessary to power a kettle.

② Here, the stainless steel counter that hosts the main food-preparation area on the rear wall of the kitchen extends all the way into a separate pantry. This kitchen is often used for large-scale entertaining, so there are times when the extra work area proves invaluable.

①

②

STORAGE

Neither space nor budget limits the provision of good storage. It's all about logic and common sense. A grand room fitted with all the very best specialized trappings and inclusions that money can buy can be outperformed by even the smallest of kitchens, provided its contents are well organized. Start by prioritizing storage in terms of frequency of use. Everything that you use regularly should be stored somewhere between eye level and hip height, making these items easy to see and relatively easy to access. The very lowest shelves and drawers should only be used for such things as baking trays, cake pans, surplus cutting boards and spare potholders: items that are used infrequently and that pose no danger to curious babies and toddlers, whether they be members of the household or visitors. The highest cabinets are a good spot for more precious objects, such as special wine glasses, platters and servingware — rarely used items that need careful storage.

Storage units can be manipulated so that they make a decorative contribution to the kitchen as well as a functional one. Here, round-cornered units suspended over islands provide open shelving, which keeps glassware readily accessible. They also have a strong impact on the quirky look of the kitchen.

Next, cluster items around the areas where they will be most useful. Everyday condiments and cooking oils should be stored near the cooktop, as should the pots and pans. Glassware benefits from a location close to the refrigerator. Pantry items should be stored close to the main food-preparation surface. Dishes are probably best stored near the surface on which meals are served, but some cooks prefer to have them close to the cooktop and oven. Other items, including food-storage containers and infrequently used small appliances, can occupy locations further away from these key work areas.

MAXIMIZING FUNCTIONAL SPACE

Standard kitchen cabinets are 24 inches (61 cm) deep, a volume that yields a good amount of storage space and results in a suitably roomy countertop. Normally, though, only those items stored at the very front of the cabinet end up being used with any regularity, while those at the back simply drift into obsolescence. For this reason, many kitchen designers favor the use of drawers over cabinets fitted with fixed shelving, even for the storage of such things as plates, servingware and pots and pans. The alternative is to install runner-mounted shelves, which have a drawer-like action; pulling out a shelf makes it easy to see and access every item within the cabinet. Runner-mounted shelves need a rim or rail to contain the items in case they lurch when pushed or pulled with too much force.

When installing a kitchen composed of stock standard cabinets, chances are you'll be left with a few odd nooks of wall space. Speak to your supplier about customized units that will make these spaces functional. For example, cabinetry could be aligned so that the "leftover" strip of space falls next to the range, where it can be fitted with a couple of shelves for the storage of baking trays, or next to the sink, where it could be fitted with a unit of pull-out hanging rods for dish towels.

❶ Shelves that are only half as wide as the base cabinets above which they are installed leave plenty of room for the work surfaces, ensuring they remain functional.

❶

❷ This simple and well-organized kitchen incorporates a full-height pantry, storage slots for baking trays and open shelving for glassware and coffee cups.

❸ A hanging-rail system with sophisticated accessories makes the most of the space between base and wall cabinets.

❹ A series of storage units runs right along the countertop in this kitchen, making full use of even the shortened wall height underneath a staircase.

❺ Good storage suits the particular needs of the household. If entertaining is a passion, then it makes sense to allow for wine storage.

① Folding doors make it possible to leave the contents of the pantry fully exposed throughout a cooking session without the obstruction to walkways that might be caused by a series of conventional swinging doors.

①

② An open-plan kitchen offers less wall space for the provision of cabinets or shelves. Here, a bank of broad pigeonholes hangs above the boundary counter, providing a little extra storage without closing off the space.

②

The space between the bottom of the base cabinets and the floor itself can also be made useful. Commonly this gap is fitted with a toeboard, a simple strip of laminate, wood or steel that conceals the supporting legs of the cabinets. It is possible, though, to have the cabinets cantilevered or wall hung so that supporting legs are not required. This means that you can install drawers in the toeboard area. Drawers that spring open with just the nudge of a toe are the most convenient, popping open to reveal their contents at a glance.

The wall between base units and wall-hung units can also yield storage space. Some manufacturers specialize in hanging-rail systems that can be fitted to kitchen walls. The basic unit is a long rod, usually made of stainless steel. Hooks from which to hang pots, pans and utensils are the most common accessory, but the range also includes paper-towel dispensers, napkin holders, spice racks and more, all of which hang from the rail, providing ready access while keeping the countertop clear.

Wall space can also be utilized by other fixtures, as long as they don't hinder the work space or encroach on headroom. Basically, while you need the full 24-inch (61-cm) depth at counter height, where your hands are working, you don't necessarily need all the available depth up higher. The area immediately below wall-hung cabinets can be used for storage of smaller items, such as coffee cups, drinking glasses or spices, without obscuring sight lines or cramping the work space. Cup hooks are an obvious example, though they tend to look a little old-fashioned in the modern kitchen. A narrow shelf fitted just below the wall-hung units offers a more streamlined solution, providing open and accessible storage without intruding on the work space. Try to limit these extrusions to a maximum depth of about 4 inches (10 cm).

PURPOSE-DESIGNED INCLUSIONS

The pull-out pantry is one of the most popular additions to
basic cabinetry. These pantries are thinner than a standard
cabinet and usually stand full height, from the floor to the
top of the wall cabinets. The pantry door pulls out to reveal
shelves accessible from either side. The narrow, pull-out format
means that groceries are never lost in the dim, dark reaches of
the back of an ordinary cupboard and though you may have to
bend to access items on the lower shelves, you'll never have to
get down on the floor in an effort to reach the goods you want.

Narrow shelves are likewise advantageous in walk-in pantries.
Shelves no more than a hand span deep can be stocked with
glasses and groceries, making it easy to see all those items at

❶ Glass-fronted storage plays an aesthetic
role in this kitchen, contributing to its chic
look. Glass also contributes a sense of depth,
a design device that gives a small kitchen
some visual breathing space.

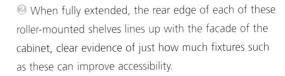

② When fully extended, the rear edge of each of these roller-mounted shelves lines up with the facade of the cabinet, clear evidence of just how much fixtures such as these can improve accessibility.

③ The advantage of open shelving is that all items remain on view, easy to locate and access. The disadvantage is that, unless you are vigilant about keeping the shelves in an orderly fashion, the whole kitchen can look permanently messy.

④ An awkward short wall is fully exploited in this kitchen, being transformed into a multi-purpose storage bank. At counter height, an appliance garage contains items that would otherwise clutter the work surface. Above it are slots for wine, and above that a closed cabinet for the storage of precious, special-occasion tableware.

a single glance. Such an approach also means that a walk-in pantry can be installed in a space not much more than 4 or 5 feet (1.2 or 1.5 m) wide.

The proliferation of small electrical appliances for making coffee, bread, toasted sandwiches, ice cream and waffles, let alone the more standard appliances, such as blenders and toasters, has seen the emergence of the appliance garage, also known as a "tambour." This unit usually occupies the space between the counter and the overhanging wall cabinets. Electrical outlets in the back wall power the appliances. If the unit is faced with a set of folding doors or a roller door, they can be completely retracted, so that when appliances are in use the area becomes just another expanse of countertop. If it is large enough, this space can also be used to store coffee cups and teaspoons, sugar bowls and bread boxes. When the activity is completed and the doors are closed, the front of the unit blends seamlessly with the surrounding cabinetry. The appliance garage lets you keep all those frequently used kitchen tools close at hand, a facility that may encourage you to use those items more often — making homemade bread a daily rather than a monthly treat, for instance. It's also an excellent way of keeping clutter off the main work surfaces and containing accessories that can otherwise sprawl right across the kitchen, especially in a family situation.

It would be impossible to list all the innovative fixtures available from kitchen cabinet manufacturers: they are many in number and new ideas are constantly being developed. Good-quality fixtures tend to be expensive, but such things as deep drawers fitted with buffers for the storage of china or pigeonholes for delicate glassware, purpose-built bread boxes and wire-mesh vegetable drawers can be a satisfyingly functional indulgence if the budget allows.

❶ Pantries function best when shelves are narrow, so that each individual item is immediately visible. The floor area of a walk-in pantry can usefully be employed as a resting place for a trolley, which can be called into action as an extra work surface in the kitchen.

❶

❷ A suspended unit faced on both sides with clear glass is a neat way of introducing additional storage space to an open-plan kitchen without inhibiting the free-flowing style of the space or obstructing sight lines.

❷

EATING AND SEATING

The last few decades of the 20th century saw the barriers of the kitchen broken down, both literally and figuratively. No longer a place where wife and mother toils in isolation for the benefit of her family or guests, the modern kitchen has become a multipurpose room accommodating functional and recreational activities. Adults station themselves in the kitchen to make phone calls, organize bill payments or catch up on the news over a pot of coffee and a muffin. Teenagers use it as a place to gather with friends, pulling together an easy snack before heading off to a movie or after coming home from school. And smaller kids gravitate there to be close to parents, finishing off homework, playing with toys or helping out with some of the simpler tasks of food preparation as family meals are made.

The open-plan kitchen is at the vanguard of this change, embodying spaces for cooking, eating and relaxing in the one, united room. Really, though, all a kitchen needs is an area of horizontal space away from the main work sites, which can function as eating area, meeting place and paperwork zone, in order to achieve a similar level of flexibility and sociability. Generously proportioned rooms can be graced with a welcoming, freestanding table setting, but even the tiniest of kitchens can usually find room for a petite breakfast bar and a stool on which to perch.

EATING ZONES

Along with the various workstations that are built into the design of a kitchen, the floorplan can also be manipulated to include an eating zone. In most cases, this is best located on the outer edge of the kitchen so that snackers and chatters don't get under the feet of the cook.

❶ The decorative potential of stools is often overlooked. This custom-made piece incorporates a collection of volcanic rocks.

❶

❷ Access to the last unit in a run of cabinetry is always slightly hindered by the proximity of the wall. In this kitchen, it was decided to acknowledge that limitation and make the most of it by installing a slim countertop from one end unit to another on the facing wall. The cabinets can still be used for storage, but only for items that are used infrequently. ❷

If possible, position the eating area so that it is handy to the refrigerator and the microwave oven. Better yet, locate it on a bank of cabinetry that includes an appliance garage equipped with toaster and coffee maker. Grouping the eating zone together with the relevant appliances creates a self-sufficient area where family members can drift in and out, catering for themselves without disturbing the work of the cook.

Strictly speaking, a counter would have to be 30–36 inches (75–92 cm) deep in order to function both as a surface for food preparation and as a place to sit with a cup of coffee and a newspaper. Any less and the two activities would be vying for space. A common configuration is to install standard 24-inch (61-cm) cabinets and top them with an extra-large countertop, with the overhang serving as the eating surface under which stools —and legs — are tucked. The minimum depth is particularly important if the countertop in question

❶ On a long but slim island counter, tall chairs are tucked under an overhang to form an eating zone at one end, while the other end, which incorporates a kitchen sink, is used as a work area.

❶

❷ Seating is arranged along two edges of this large, granite-topped island, on the sides farthest away from the main work areas.

❷

① This open-plan space incorporates a variety of eating areas: a simple breakfast bar at the island counter, a family dining table and an outdoor setting on the sheltered deck.

①

② A lowered counter provides a casual eating area for adults but really comes into its own as a special place for children in the kitchen. The child-friendly height makes this a surface that can be used for meals, for play, perhaps for homework or just for the fun of lending a hand with simple cooking activities.

②

is a single, flat surface. Without any clear demarcation between zones, the tools and products of the work surface and the coffee cups, car keys, schoolbooks and reading glasses of the eating surface tend to drift across into each other's domain, to the dissatisfaction of individuals on both sides of the counter.

An extended depth is less important if the counter is long, say 6 feet (1.8 m) or more. The extra length means that stools or chairs can be mustered at a distance from the main activity center, be it a sink, a cooktop or a main food-preparation site.

Raised or lowered strip counters, commonly known as breakfast bars, are a more clearly defined way of installing an eating zone. The change in height between the main counter and the breakfast bar counter makes it clear where the activity and paraphernalia of one zone should end and the other begin. If a mixing bowl appears on the raised counter, or a handbag on the work surface, it's a clear-cut case of trespass.

Using a contrasting surface material for the breakfast bar further emphasizes the different functions of the two counters, and offers opportunities for some interesting textural juxtapositions. It can also be a practical decision. For example, while stainless steel is an excellent and effective work surface, its cold, hard touch is incompatible with the less physically demanding tasks of serving a snack or sorting through the mail. Far better to make a switch, using wood or laminate for the breakfast bar.

TABLE SETTINGS

The kitchen table has always been a feature of the rambling, country kitchen and remains a beloved inclusion wherever there is room to accommodate it. Traditionally, the kitchen table was centrally located and served as an extra food-preparation surface outside meal times. The fact that the table can be used in this way is what justifies its presence in a modern kitchen, even where space is a little tight. If there genuinely isn't room for a freestanding table, consider a small drop-down table attached to the wall.

Because the kitchen table is likely to be used for many purposes — doubling as a work surface, becoming an ad hoc desk for children and their homework or adults and their tax returns, and being the setting for informal meals that involve family members and guests of all ages — it, and its chairs, must be robust and easy to clean. A strong, wooden table is the obvious choice: it will tolerate knocks and scratches and look all the better for them a few years down the track. Laminated surfaces are easy to keep clean, but will show signs of wear after a while. Stone- and glass-topped tables are both durable, but tend to be cold to the touch and therefore a little uncomfortable to dine at. Avoid upholstered chairs, because spills and stains are inevitable in this environment. Consider tie-on cushions to soften a hard chair or loose covers to protect a padded seat.

❶ Poised at the end of a peninsula, close to the door and near to a pantry and a refrigerator, this circular eating area has the look of a smart bistro.

❶

❷ The granite work surface of this kitchen actually wraps around the cabinetry to the exterior of the room, forming an eating zone on the edges of an informal living space. A collection of cookbooks is stored in the glass-fronted cabinets, making this a pleasant spot to sit and dream up a dinner menu over a cup of coffee.   ❷

❶ This breakfast bar was designed to have qualities that would give it a distinctive aesthetic role even when not in use as an eating area. Downlights mounted on the underside of the overhang are there purely to make a feature of the facade of the island counter: a panel of sandblasted glass over a rosewood veneer.

❷ The contrast between the weathered surface of a vintage wooden table and the sleek molded plastic of contemporary dining chairs is visually dynamic.

LIGHTING

A plan for kitchen lighting must be finalized early in the project as most of the installation of electrical wiring, light fittings and light switches will have to be completed before cabinets, counters, appliances and, in some cases, wall and floor finishes are put in place. The scheme must include both task lighting and ambient lighting. Task lighting ensures that the functional areas — the work surfaces where food is prepared, the range where meals are cooked, the countertops where meals are served and the sink where cleaning activities are conducted — are all well lit. Ambient lighting, on the other hand, provides illumination at a less intense level that is suitable for simple activities such as arranging flowers in a vase, unpacking the shopping or simply having a conversation over a cup of coffee.

TASK LIGHTING

The first principle of task lighting is that the cook should never cast a shadow over his or her work and that means never locating a light source behind a working cook. Working in shadow strains the eyes and can make an inherently risky activity — using a cutting board or cooking on a hot plate — even more dangerous.

The challenge, then, is to position light sources where they will shine directly onto work surfaces. Downlights — either surface-mounted or recessed into the ceiling — are ideal, tracklights even more so, given that they can be shifted if your theoretical lighting plan reveals some shortcomings when actually put to work. Tracklights also reduce installation costs: multiple lamps are attached to a single set of tracks, so only one connection is required for every three, four or five lights. A disadvantage of surface-mounted downlights and tracklights

❶ Hoods are an unavoidable obstruction to ceiling-mounted lights. Fortunately, many manufacturers produce quality fittings that incorporate task lighting for the cooktop.

❷ Tracklights are a simple way to furnish a kitchen with multiple lamps, which can be directed at numerous sites across the room. The curved fixture, which mirrors the shape of the curved island, is an example of how easily tracklights can be customized to suit the style and shape of a kitchen. **❷**

is that they will attract dust and grease and therefore will need regular cleaning, unlike recessed downlights, which sit flush with the ceiling and present no grime-attracting surface area.

Pendant lights can also be used as task lights, provided that they are located well away from heat sources, such as the cooktop: the high temperatures may cause the shades to crack. You should also avoid hanging them so high that their light is dispersed, rendering them useless as a source of focused task lighting. Pendant lights can look striking over a peninsula or island and can do a lot to establish the style of a kitchen: oversized tin shades in an industrial kitchen, cylindrical wood-veneer shades in a retro kitchen, checked fabric shades in a country kitchen — all of these contribute much in the way of character. Tiny, contemporary halogen light fittings can look smart when fixed over a counter that runs along a wall, but if the light shades are too bulky, the area will look cramped.

A strategically positioned series of recessed downlights provides excellent illumination throughout the kitchen. Simple pendant lights above the island function as task lighting for the work surface as required, and can also be used to transform the mood of the room at the flick of a switch. When the counter is used for a casual meal, the pendant lights remain on, casting a warm pool of light over the setting, while ceiling lights are switched off, causing the rest of the work space to recede into shadows.

①

① Ceiling lights can be used to illuminate a counter that also serves as an informal eating area, though their utilitarian character can often discourage social activity. Pendant lights are a more familiar sight and serve to distinguish such a zone from the more functional areas of the kitchen.

②

If fixing pendant lights over a work surface that will double as a casual eating place, remember to have dimmers fitted so that the strong illumination suitable for food preparation can be reduced to an atmospheric glow for late-night suppers.

Lighting a work surface adequately when there are wall-hung cabinets installed above the counter is a slightly more complex matter. If the kitchen ceiling is not too high, and if the wall cabinets are no more than half the depth of the base cabinets — a common ratio — then ceiling-mounted downlights positioned in line with the face of those overhead units will cast light on the counter below. Obviously, such an approach results in a reasonable level of illumination for the front half of the counter, but the section close to the wall will be in shadow. This may be acceptable in an area where meals are served or coffee is made, but it is not ideal and is best avoided in the

② Cabinetry suspended over an island or peninsula can obstruct task lighting from ceiling-mounted fittings. The best solution is to install downlights into the underside of the units themselves.

③ Uplights mounted discreetly along the inside edges of a ceiling recess create a subtle wash of light. This unusual arrangement makes for a sleek and understated form of ambient lighting in a smoothly styled kitchen.

③

primary work areas. An effective, though rather expensive, alternative is to have downlights installed in the underside of the wall-mounted cabinets. Some kitchen cabinet suppliers offer units of this kind in their standard ranges.

Fluorescent striplights are a cheaper and easier option for installation under wall cabinets. Being located around eye level, striplights can be a source of glare. If possible, have them mounted close to the outer edge of the cabinet, angled back in toward the wall and shielded by a baffle or cornice.

Ceiling-mounted downlights, tracklights and fluorescent strip lighting are all suitable for a walk-in pantry. Ask your electrician to install a door-activated switch so that the light comes on automatically whenever you enter the pantry.

❶ Recessed downlights and streamlined tracklight fittings are discreet, but pendant lights can play a decorative role. These metal shades tip the style balance of this elegant room, playing up its chic industrial character.

❷ This nostalgic fitting plays a functional role, but perhaps has greater significance in setting the mood of an eclectic kitchen that marries modern cabinetry and appliances with vintage pieces.

❸ A combination of artificial lighting and well-positioned natural light sources results in a kitchen that is well lit at all times without unnecessary consumption of energy resources. Here, daylight entering through a paneled window is augmented by a pair of skylights.

① Natural light entering through glazed ceiling panels and framed glass doors balances the brooding tendency of dark-chocolate-toned cabinetry. At night, low-voltage pendant lights and tracklights sparkle, imbuing those richly colored wood surfaces with sophisticated glamour.

② When natural light is in good supply, no other means of illumination is necessary during the day. In this family kitchen, a set of canopy windows furnishes the primary food-preparation surface with light throughout the day.

③ Privacy issues don't necessarily prohibit the use of windows. One solution is to use sandblasted or acid-etched glass that allows filtered light to enter without compromising the privacy of the household. Another is to install clear glass windows above head height, as shown in this kitchen. The windows allow daylight to penetrate but eliminate the possibility of anyone seeing into the kitchen from outside or anyone inside the house looking directly out onto a neighboring property.

①

②

③

AMBIENT LIGHTING

Always include the facility for the kitchen to be lit at a level that makes it easy to grab a glass of water or collect a snack from the refrigerator without necessarily activating the full strength of the task lighting. This could be done by assigning a set of downlights or tracklights to a single switch, by installing a couple of simple pendant lights or wall-mounted uplights, or by having dimmers fitted to the task-specific lights so they can be used at reduced strength.

If one of the kitchen counters is to be used as a casual eating area, it should be serviced with a level of illumination compatible with that relaxed and social activity. Either fit dimmers to the task lighting used in the area or allow for additional fittings that provide a softer light. Rise and fall fittings, which can be pulled down close to the work surface when food preparation is in full swing, or lifted away to provide a more dispersed light during mealtimes, are also a good choice.

❶ In this soaring space, recessed ceiling lights would have been virtually useless. Instead, tracklights suspended from the high ceiling furnish the work surfaces with light.

❷ Natural light is highly desirable but clear glass windows can present privacy problems. Here, frosted panels supply a filtered light without exposing the interior to public view.

❸ Reflective surfaces can be used to enhance light sources. Here, light falling on stainless steel illuminates the work zone but also brightens a dramatically dark room.

9

FIXTURES

Cabinets and counters, work zones and storage areas, lighting and color: these are the building blocks of the kitchen, the elements that ensure the floorplan functions efficiently, that the work of the cook can be carried out effectively and that the space contributes something to the household in terms of character and mood.

CABINETS

Like no other room in the house, the modern kitchen has been standardized. The vast majority are fitted with built-in cabinets, most of which are standard, mass-produced units made from medium-density fiberboard or a similar composite material. The huge numbers in which these cabinets are produced means they can be sold at very reasonable prices.

More expensive are fitted kitchens made from solid wood. The wooden construction makes for a more durable base unit, but it must be appropriately dried and acclimatized to interior conditions or it may warp and move, thus undermining the stability of the whole kitchen.

There is an alternative to the built-in kitchen, one used for centuries in American and European kitchens and still employed in rural kitchens around the world. It's the so-called "unfitted" kitchen, made up of freestanding items of furniture. Its non-standard nature is both an attraction and a drawback, producing kitchens of personal and distinctive style, yet raising problems in terms of finding pieces that fulfill the functions or match the dimensions of a given kitchen. The search for the perfect pieces might be a chore for some, but others will relish the odyssey. Freestanding cabinets, dressers and pantries are easily maneuvered into place, but installing appliances and plumbing into vintage furniture — dropping a sink into an old side table, for example — requires the assistance of a tradesperson who is not only skilled but who shares your enthusiasm for the unorthodox task.

A 21st-century version of the traditional freestanding kitchen is currently emerging, attracting particular popularity in Europe. Aesthetically, it bridges the gap between the fitted

PREVIOUS PAGES Simple, clean-lined wooden cabinets give an organic warmth to spaces with a pared-back, contemporary form.

❶

❶ Concealed behind a drawer front, this pull-out surface can serve as an extra chopping area or as a very compact eating spot.

❷ Touch-sensitive mechanisms make it easy to use a cabinet or inspect the contents of a drawer even when hands are holding a hot pan or a couple of shopping bags. They also give a streamlined look, as the facade is not punctuated by door handles or drawer pulls.

❸ Modern hand-forged knobs and handles give this new kitchen a vintage charm.

❹ In this kitchen, the presence of an island meant that counter space around the cooktop could be sacrificed for storage, in the form of floor-to-ceiling cabinetry.

❺ Here, the mobile island creates a shifting boundary between the kitchen and a living area. The pendant lights that mark its usual resting place can be retracted as necessary.

and the unfitted kitchen, consisting of a series of essentially uniform modular units — usually faced in either solid wood or stainless steel and typically mounted on wheels — that can be arranged and rearranged in a variety of ways. Obviously this concept comes into its own in the open spaces of modern warehouse conversions, but the adaptability of the units can be utilized even in a traditional home. For instance, a unit fitted with an under-counter refrigerator could be wheeled onto a deck and used as a bar during a social gathering, its power cord being plugged into an external outlet. Or a section that incorporated a microwave oven could be installed in a guest bedroom suite for the duration of a visitor's stay, then returned to the main kitchen. The design of the units might also incorporate interchangeable countertops, so that, for example, a laminated inset in one unit could be swapped with the marble inset in another when the cook requires a pastry-making surface close to the oven.

❶

❷ An important element of the concept is that these kitchens can be taken with you when you move from one house to another, reducing the need for you to spend time and money redesigning the kitchen in your new home, or adjusting to a design that doesn't suit your personal needs.

THE BASIC UNIT

Far and away the most common and most economical kitchen cabinetry is made up of a basic fiberboard framework fitted with fiberboard doors with a laminate or wood veneer, solid wooden doors, or doors with panels of glass or steel — an extensive array of options for a virtually limitless variety of decorative looks. The standardized nature of the units makes it easy to update an existing kitchen or to refurbish and personalize a kitchen in a newly acquired property, simply by removing old doors and drawer fronts and replacing them

③

with new ones. This point is worth emphasizing, in part because of the economy and flexibility it represents but also to reinforce that there is no need to remove solid, functioning frameworks when you want a new look.

There are drawbacks to the standardized sizing of mass-produced cabinetry framing. The inherent limitations can impinge on your floorplan and possibly even make it harder to arrive at design solutions for an unusually proportioned room. And while most manufacturers produce units in a small range of widths and perhaps two different depths, more often than not they offer only one standardized height. This can be a problem for anyone markedly smaller or taller than average and may even make the kitchen uncomfortable to use. If these

❶ A wall of storage is faced with stainless steel door fronts. Stainless steel is prone to messy fingermarks, but the long door handles should minimize the problem.

❷ Lattice-fronted cabinets give a lightweight look to this kitchen, with the added benefit that they improve the ventilation of their interiors. The extra air flow is of particular advantage in a humid climate.

❸ Brilliant blue appliances are a standout feature of this wood-veneer kitchen. The contrast is emphasized by the cobalt-blue, lacquer finish of two pot drawers below the cooktop, a pair of pull-out pantries and the uprights that frame the island.

restraints represent insurmountable obstacles for you and your kitchen, then you should consider a custom-made kitchen. The expense will be greater, but the resulting cabinetry will meet your needs to a satisfyingly precise degree.

The standard base unit measures 36 inches (92 cm) high and 24 inches (61 cm) deep. Rolling pastry, kneading dough and other similar tasks should be carried out on a lower surface so the cook can lean over and apply weight to the work. Many suppliers also offer a unit 30 inches (76 cm) high for this purpose. Wall-hung cabinets tend to be around half the depth of the base units to make headroom for the cook. There is no point in installing 24-inch (61-cm) deep wall units over the same depth base units: the counter will be very difficult to use. If it is possible to dispense with a work surface on a given wall, then extract maximum storage space by installing solid cabinetry from floor to ceiling.

DOORS AND DRAWER FRONTS

Wooden doors and drawer fronts vary in hue from the pale blond of ash and beech to the darker tones of cherry wood and oak, and in grain from the heavily knotted pine to the ornamental burring of walnut. And they can present as a frameless panel of wood, as tongue-and-groove paneled doors or as framed doors supporting insets of glass, tin, wire mesh or other materials.

Aluminum strips give a sleek edge to black laminated cabinetry. Glass-fronted wall cabinets balance the effect of the deliberately bold and graphic floor cabinets. The lower level of the peninsula forms a casual eating area but is also at the right height for weight-bearing tasks, such as rolling pastry.

Wood-veneer door and drawer fronts, made by fixing a super-thin layer of real wood onto a core of fiberboard, make it possible to enjoy the look of exotic woods that would otherwise be far too expensive to use. They can also be used to give a wood finish to unusually shaped units, such as curved corner cabinets.

Plywood is a fashionable alternative within the wood category. It is a material composed of layers of pine, structured so that the grain runs in alternating directions from one layer to the next. This construction gives plywood superior structural stability and also produces an attractive striped effect on cut ends, a decorative detail that can be used to great effect and gives a contemporary edge to a traditional material. Plywood comes in different grades: the higher the grade, the fewer knots appear in the material, a factor that contributes greater stability and a more uniform finish. The most reliable for use in the kitchen is marine-grade plywood, a material tried and tested in the demanding environments of seagoing vessels.

❶ Suspended from the ceiling, this open-sided unit of solid kauri pine serves two purposes. It displays a collection of vases, but it also furnishes the island with task lighting. Wiring runs up into the ceiling through the stainless steel supports.

❷ Super-thin veneers of real wood can be applied over curved surfaces to give a solid wood look to some unusual cabinet shapes.

❸ Stable, durable and organic, plywood is a competitively priced alternative to solid wood.

❶

❶ Wall cabinets provide extensive storage in this kitchen. Had they been faced with solid door fronts, the look would have been overwhelming and oppressive, but pale and luminous glass doors are far less obtrusive.

❷ A paint finish was applied to these solid wooden doors, achieving an aged look appropriate to the kitchen's location within an old sandstone house.

❸ Custom-made cabinetry permits an enviable degree of detail that suits the style of this kitchen. Here, slide-out column units frame the sink and provide secure storage for cleaning products. Nearby, a matching pair frames the range and stores spices and oils.

Door and drawer fronts made by fixing a thin veneer of plastic to a core of fiberboard are commonly referred to as laminated surfaces. The range of plain color and patterned laminates available literally runs into the thousands, making it easy to achieve a very personalized look in the kitchen. An even greater degree of personalization is available with the computer technology employed by some manufacturers, which makes it possible to print laminates with your own photographs or artworks. Such an individualized treatment attracts a premium price, but in general the cost of standard laminated surfaces is very reasonable.

Fiberboard cores can also be overlaid with sheets of metal. Stainless steel is the most popular, offering the streamlined, industrial look highly prized in many kitchens. Copper, brass and zinc are alternatives and can be used to create a quirky, vintage effect. Some manufacturers of laminates produce look-alikes that allow you to replicate the style of metal without the expense or the sometimes tricky maintenance.

Paint can be used on either solid wooden doors or fiberboard cores, although the paintwork must be of top quality if the surfaces are to withstand the humidity, grease and general wear and tear of the kitchen. If doing the work yourself, be sure to use the appropriate primer and finish with an oil-based gloss paint. The gloss will be an easier surface to clean, while the oil base offers superior durability. The commercial version is the so-called "lacquered" surface, made by spray-painting multiple layers to produce a very stable, very durable finish.

You can also opt to leave the fiberboard cores exposed, simply sealing and finishing the surface for a budget-priced, warm yet contemporary look.

Don't feel that you have to limit yourself to one kind of material for your door and drawer fronts. Using a variety of treatments increases the decorative potential of the kitchen. For example, affordable laminate can be coaxed into some quite imaginative and sophisticated outcomes simply by varying the colors and patterns used throughout the kitchen, perhaps by setting an ice-blue island against a backdrop of chocolate-toned wall-fixed cabinetry, or facing alternating surfaces with pink and cherry red or bright blue and white in a cheerful family kitchen.

Varying the materials can also aid design solutions. Using solid wooden doors on base units and glass doors on wall-hung units, for example, can reduce the visual impact of the upper cabinets, an important consideration in smaller spaces or rooms with low ceilings.

②

③

ISLANDS

The freestanding island has become a standard feature in the contemporary kitchen. To some extent it is a descendant of the traditional country kitchen table, a well-worn, much-loved, centrally located piece of furniture used as a meeting place, a venue for family meals and a handy work surface for all kinds of household duties. The island of the domestic kitchen is also influenced by the structure of the professional kitchen, where spatial efficiency is crucial. Commercial kitchens often sport a large central countertop where many cooks are able to work at once, each turning their hand to a particular task without getting in the way of the others or crossing the path of the person focusing on hot pans or juggling dirty dishes at the sink. Seen from these two perspectives, the island clearly has both a social and functional role to play.

Counter space is limited on the intensively equipped rear wall of the kitchen, so this freestanding island counter must provide as much horizontal work space as possible. Locating the kitchen sink here is an expense, but facilitates the island's function as the main site for food preparation. An overhang on the outer edge of the island provides space for simple stools, making it possible for the counter to also serve as a casual eating area.

FORM AND FUNCTION

The fundamental contribution of the island is counter space. Positioned centrally in the kitchen, it immediately provides a food-preparation surface that can be accessed from any side and by more than one person at a time. This makes it almost essential in the modern kitchen, where meal preparation is often the work of multiple cooks. The island increases the available counter space for the appliances in its vicinity, the most obvious example being the range, where surfaces to either side of the cooktop are supplemented by those of the island directly behind the cook. A gap of at least 4 feet (1.2 m) between the island and the facing appliance or cabinetry is essential if two people are to work in the same area at once.

An island mounted on wheels obviously has the advantage of being transportable: pull it close to the oven when baking

❶ Here, an island is overhung with a storage unit that matches the curve of the cabinetry below. The vacant space above and below the unit prevents the arrangement from looking too congested.

❷ The limited counter space of this one-wall kitchen is supplemented by a generously sized island that doubles as an eating area. The make-up of the unit — maple and white laminated cabinetry overlaid with a thick slab of sandblasted glass — has a furnished look that allows it to comfortably occupy a transitional zone between the kitchen and the adjacent living area.

❸ A utility sink ensures that this island can function as a work surface independent of the washing-up area on the far wall.

is in progress, close to the sink when cleaning up after a party, or use it as a buffet table by wheeling it into the dining area.

Even something as simple as a table can function as an island in this context, offering plenty of surface space, while also providing leg room for anyone who wants to pull up a stool. Tables, however, are set at a lower height than the standard countertops, so the ergonomic conditions are not ideal. Then there's the issue of storage: very few kitchens can afford to give up floorspace without some gain in storage capacity.

For that reason, islands are very often freestanding versions of the fitted wall cabinets. If the island is to function as a place where people can sit to work or eat, then there must be some provision for legroom: an extended countertop will provide the required overhang. Depending on its size and on the customs of the kitchen, an island can be used to house pantry items, cookware, fresh vegetables, table linen or cookbooks.

❶ Ceiling-mounted ventilation units, which are required when a cooktop is installed in an island, can be overwhelmingly obtrusive in a small or streamlined space. In this rambling family kitchen, however, the hood simply adds to the busy, buzzy look.

❷ Positioned within a U-shaped kitchen, this island's functional independence is emphasized by a complete break in style.

❸ Slabs of stone seem to fold up and over the surface of this island. It's an elegant effect that smooths out the intrusiveness of the island in an otherwise streamlined space. It also neatly contains the seating area.

Islands do not have to match the surrounding cabinetry. Nor do they have to match the dimensions of conventional cabinetry. Consider the various purposes the island is to serve and make choices accordingly. If it is to be used as a base for making bread or pastry, a marble counter set at a lower height of around 30 inches (76 cm) will provide a surface tailor-made for the heavy weight-bearing tasks of kneading and rolling. If bread making or pastry making is a regular activity, but the island will be used most often for simple food preparation, then consider a custom-made, split-level unit. If large-scale entertaining is a frequent occurrence and the island functions primarily as a base from which to serve meals, then ensure that the counter is sized to accommodate eight or ten dinner plates with ease. Unlike the wall cabinetry, which serves a fairly basic function as storage space, the island is a unit that exists specifically to meet the particular requirements of the cook and the kitchen.

Island counters can be used to clearly define the work space of the kitchen in an open-plan area, as was the case here. The unusual tumbled marble facing of the body of the island is an aesthetic link with the tumbled marble paving of a nearby courtyard.

① Here, a well-used butcher's block has been adapted to serve as an island in a modern kitchen with casual country charm.

② Topping standard-width cabinets with an extra-deep countertop provides enough overhang for a simple eating area with stools.

③ Installing a utility sink at one end of an island can be an expensive and troublesome process. It does, however, allow the island to be a fully functional food-preparation area even when the primary kitchen sink is in use. It also means that other family members can grab a drink or fill the coffee pot without straying into the main body of the kitchen when the cook is busy.

APPLIANCES

It is increasingly common for islands to accommodate utility sinks — a faucet and basin set apart from the main cleaning sink and dedicated to food-preparation tasks, such as the rinsing of vegetables. The utility sink is generally better located to one end of an island rather than in the middle so as not to prevent the island from functioning as a casual eating spot.

In some kitchens, the island is such a focal point that it comes close to constituting a kitchen in its own right. Ranges, full-size sinks, dishwashers, under-counter refrigerators and microwave ovens are regularly installed in island units in open-plan kitchens, giving cooks the opportunity to face toward the living area no matter what task they are working at.

Such well-appointed islands present considerable problems in terms of installation and maintenance. They must be serviced by plumbing and electrical wiring extending from the wall, under the floor and up through the base of the unit. This is easy enough to achieve in new building work, but harder in refurbishments, as the removal of the existing floor is an unavoidable part of the procedure. The design must also address the issue of ongoing maintenance, incorporating some form of reasonably easy access to pipes and wires in case of future repair work.

Including a cooktop in an island also necessitates installing a ventilation unit of some kind. It is possible to hang a hood from the ceiling, but installation is more difficult than the standard wall-mounted application and therefore usually more expensive. There's also the problem that the overhanging canopy is a rather massive visual obstruction and will undo any attempts to create a loose, free-flowing space. A good alternative is to opt for counter-mounted ventilation units that sit close to the cooktop.

❷

❸

SURFACES

The walls, the floor, the counters: each and every surface in the kitchen bears the brunt of hard work and high traffic. This is one decorating decision in which practicality must come before personal taste. Make sure the material you choose is a suitable match for the conditions, then move on to the more stimulating considerations of color, pattern, style and texture.

COUNTERTOPS

A kitchen countertop is possibly the most hardworking surface in a house and, as a consequence, high standards are demanded of the materials used to make it. They must, for example, be waterproof and resistant to mold and mildew. They must be hardwearing. They must be easy to clean with soap and water rather than chemicals that may linger and later be absorbed by food. Heat-resistance is an advantage. The best countertops are able to withstand the heat of pots and pans taken straight from the cooktop or oven, while others can be supplemented with special heatproof mats.

They must also stand up to the particular punishment of food preparation — the cutting edge of the knife and the acidic splashes of such ingredients as vinegar and lemon juice — and present a non-porous surface unlikely to harbor bacteria.

Laminates are commonly used as countertops in the kitchen. Formerly, the thin plastic laminate, which is bonded to a core of chipboard or medium-density fiberboard, was available in only a narrow range of solid colors. These days, hundreds if not thousands of plain colors are on offer along with a similar number of patterns. Advanced computer technology allows some manufacturers to print laminates with your own photographs or artworks, a process that can be expensive but yields brilliantly idiosyncratic results. The main attractions of the basic laminates are low price, wide availability and ease of installation. They will scratch if used as a cutting surface, so use cutting boards instead. Hot pots and pans will burn the surface. Spills left for any length of time may leave a stain, particularly on older countertops, where the glossy surface has worn down. Moisture can get in under the laminate, loosening the adhesive and causing the plastic surface to come away from the chipboard core. As insurance against such a mishap, ensure you use a quality product and an experienced installer and consider asking for a rolled drip edge and even an integrated backsplash to reduce the number of seams.

Wood is another reasonably priced option for countertops. The warm hues and rich grain of wooden countertops bring a softer element to a space. They are, however, prone to water damage, easily burned and susceptible to cracks and warping

PREVIOUS PAGES The countertop surrounding a sink must be waterproof. Timber and laminate, properly prepared and installed, can be used in such a situation, but materials such as stainless steel and stone offer a far more reliable option.

❶ Throughout this kitchen, a set of pull-out timber counters was installed just below the top drawer of the base units, effectively doubling the counter space.

❷ Like timber, concrete is a material that can be used to different effect in different environments. It can look edgy and modern in an urban kitchen space, but its stony finish also complements organic materials such as wood.

❸ A change in material signifies a change in function. Here, stainless steel is used for the main work surface, while granite forms an angled breakfast bar.

❹ This kitchen features a concrete counter with a clearly visible aggregate. Concrete can, however, be produced in a finer finish or even tinted to produce less rugged, more sophisticated outcomes.

in the dry air of a heated house. Wood must be properly cured before it is installed; unscrupulous businesses will use "green" wood rather than taking the time to let the wood dry properly, so ask your supplier about their standard procedures. For greater reliability, the countertop should be sealed both top and bottom. Oil-based sealers are preferable and should be re-applied every couple of years, or more regularly if the counter is being used as a cutting surface.

Solid surfaces, made by blending natural minerals into acrylic or resin, are produced by a number of manufacturers and tend to be marketed under their brand names, including Corian. They can be molded or milled into a variety of shapes so that a run of countertop can incorporate an integrated sink or cutting board, for example. They are non-porous, which makes them resistant to stains and mold. Because they are solid and the color is constant throughout the depth of the material, any light scratches or burns can be sanded out.

Aside from its handsome gleam, polished granite is valued for its impressive resilience to moisture, heat, scratching and staining. It is, however, very heavy; check that your cabinets can carry the load before installing a granite countertop.

Marble, unlike granite, is susceptible to stains. If you're reluctant to commit to extreme vigilance in wiping up drips, then you must have the surface sealed, remembering that the sealant will eventually wear away and will need re-application. Nonetheless, marble is a beautiful stone, capable of bringing grandeur to a classically styled kitchen or old-world charm to a country kitchen. Characteristically cold, marble is also beloved of cooks, being an ideal surface for pastry making.

Stainless steel is favored in professional kitchens for its high resistance to heat and moisture. Its non-porous surface also makes for an exceptionally hygienic countertop. It will scratch,

❶ Granite is usually associated with dark tones, from black to forest greens, but also comes in paler colors, such as the speckled ivory seen here. Such a counter combines the classic look of marble with the ultra-high performance of granite.

❷ Solid wooden counters are attractive, but can be affected by moisture and may warp or split. Surfaces made of a conglomerate of thick strips of wood provide greater stability.

❸ Solid-surface counters are synthetic replicas of natural materials, such as granite.

❹ Tiled countertops offer a hardwearing surface at a reasonably low cost, but they do present maintenance problems. Their grout lines tend to accumulate grime and mold and require frequent cleaning.

❺ Laminate is used for these kitchen counter-tops, but the servery is topped with wood, a more expensive material that gives a furnished look to the living-area side of the counter.

so cutting boards are essential, and abrasive cleaning products and scouring pads should be avoided. Though it is unlikely to stain, it is prone to surface smears, which can be very difficult to remove. A brushed or matte rather than a polished finish will mask the smudgy fingerprints and may even camouflage light scratches. It is possible to have stainless steel countertops custom made to incorporate sinks and drainers.

Concrete countertops are gaining in popularity, partly for their rugged industrial look and partly because they can be poured into forms that incorporate sinks and drainers, a seamless look that many find appealing. Pigments and decorative particles can be added to the concrete for an individualistic finish. It must be sealed to make it waterproof and stain resistant.

Remember that you don't have to limit yourself to a single material for countertops. For example, you could install a stainless steel countertop along one wall, incorporating a sink and a cooktop, then use wood elsewhere. You could also install contrasting materials as insets, dropping a slab of marble for pastry making into a wooden countertop, or setting a wooden cutting surface into a poured concrete countertop. Such an approach will result in work surfaces that are tailor-made for your personal requirements and enable you to use some of the more expensive materials, such as stainless steel and polished stone, even when your budget is limited.

❶ This island incorporates different types of work surfaces for different purposes. Granite is a high-quality, all-round performer, but cannot be used as a surface for cutting. Wood, on the other hand, is perfect for the task. The lowered portion of the counter is good for heavy weight-bearing activities, such as kneading and rolling.

❶

❷ On one side of the island, stainless steel provides an excellent work surface: hygienic, hardwearing, easy to clean and heat resistant — all important qualities, given that the counter incorporates a cooktop. On the other side, a concrete countertop presents a more decorative, less utilitarian aspect to the surrounding living areas.

❷

① Stainless steel comes in sheet form, which means an extended area can be covered without the need for joins. These can harbor dirt and bacteria in the moist conditions around a sink and cooktop.

② Dark ceramic tiles and a plain white grout combine for a bold and graphic look. A tinted grout would result in a more subdued finish.

③ The surfaces directly behind the cooktop and the sink are the areas that really need the extra protection of a backsplash, but most people prefer the uniformity of a wall treatment that extends right around the room. Here, a border tile adds decorative focus to the area behind the cooktop.

WALLS

The kitchen is by nature a hot and often steamy place and any wall surface must be resilient enough to handle these tough conditions. Kitchen walls are also susceptible to cooking splatters, dishwashing sloshes and a gradual buildup of grime, so they must be easy to clean and maintain.

As ever, paint is an inexpensive, easy to apply, decoratively potent option. The matte paints that look so soft and subtle elsewhere in the house are unsuitable in the kitchen: the porous surface is likely to absorb dirt and grease and before long that appealingly tactile finish becomes unappealing and irreversibly grubby. Instead, choose a semi-gloss or gloss finish, remembering that the more reflective the finish, the more it shows up the flaws in the surface of the wall. Oil-based paints, though slightly more labor-intensive to apply, are more robust than the water-based alternative and so can stand considerably more scrubbing and cleaning. Some paint manufacturers offer blends with special mold-resistant properties that are ideally suited to the kitchen; others can mix mold-resistant additives into their standard products.

Wood paneling is a popular look, particularly in spaces with a country-kitchen ambiance. If painting the wood, choose an oil-based semi-gloss or gloss-finish paint; the reflective surface will be less likely to absorb grease and dirt. If, however, you long for the warm and natural look of unpainted wood, be sure to apply a sealer to repel moisture and guard against stains.

Classic black and white tiling, ethereal glass mosaics, hand-painted tiles from Mexico or Morocco or Portugal — the decorative possibilities of tiles are virtually limitless. Glazed tiles have the advantage of being both attractive and extremely practical in the kitchen, given that they are water-resistant, mold-resistant, heat-resistant and easy to wipe clean. The porous grout between the tiles can attract mold: if you are reluctant to take on the chore of regular brushing, you can enquire about special mold-resistant grouting materials or have the entire tiled surface sealed, including the grout. Unglazed tiles absorb grime and moisture and are susceptible to stains, so are an impractical choice in the kitchen.

BACKSPLASHES
The wall area between the countertop and the bottom of the upper cabinets is known as the backsplash. Because it runs along the particularly hardworking areas behind the cooktop and the sink, it requires special attention. Like the rest of the kitchen wall surfaces, the backsplash must be water-resistant

and easy to clean but it must also have a high resistance to heat. Tiles are a safe option. Wood is most certainly not. A painted surface can work as a backsplash around a sink, but the heat given off by the cooktop is likely to make the paint blister and peel over time.

Slate, marble, granite and other stones are popular backsplash options. Those with richly veined or extravagantly patterned surfaces can look striking in a grand kitchen, but if the look of the kitchen is more subdued, make sure you request a piece with more subtle color variations.

Safety glass offers a smooth, sheer surface, very much at home in modern minimalist or industrial-style kitchens. Clear glass fixed onto a white wall surface will take on a slightly green hue, but you also have the option of having the back of the glass painted the color of your choice, so that it either blends in seamlessly with the wall color or makes a dramatic color contrast, as you choose. Note that regular glass is not at all suitable for use as a backsplash: only specially made safety glass should be used. It should also be installed by an experienced tradesperson, who will fix it to the wall without cracking or chipping the material and who will apply a sealer right around the edges to ensure that no moisture seeps in between the wall and the glass.

Possibly the hardiest of all materials for a backsplash is stainless steel. It is waterproof and mold-resistant, and can withstand high temperatures and open flames. It is essentially easy to clean, but prone to smudges and fingerprints, which can be tremendously irritating for more fastidious house-keepers. Stainless steel's suitability for the task is backed up by the fact that it is used in commercial kitchens right around the world.

❶ Glass backsplashes have a non-porous surface that makes them ideal for application behind a cooktop, but they also have a marvelous reflective quality. The reflections they capture can introduce an element of movement, a feature that has a surprisingly positive impact in a small, closed-in kitchen.

❶

❷ A wall of sandstone, once the exterior wall of this historic country house, makes a stunning backdrop for the new kitchen extension. Being extremely porous, however, it is highly unsuitable as a backsplash surface. Plain white horizontal tiles, a common treatment in 19th-century kitchens, clad the backsplash zone.

❷

FLOORS

Floors can be considered in two categories: the soft and the hard. Soft floors are made of materials that yield, while hard floors are resolutely solid. This point of difference is particularly relevant in the kitchen, where cooks can labor on their feet for hours at a time, standing in front of the cooktop or crossing backward and forward from the refrigerator to the cutting board. Wooden flooring is relatively easy on the feet, but is not technically considered one of the "soft" surfaces.

SOFT SURFACES

Linoleum is a surface in need of an image update. Sometimes confused with vinyl, which is a synthetic product, linoleum is in fact a natural material, made from a mixture of ground cork, linseed oil, wood resins and wood flour, which is then pressed onto a natural fiber backing. It's true that the linoleum floors of half a century ago were prone to cracks and splits, but those flaws have been more or less eliminated in the modern product. Linoleum is durable and easy to keep clean, although special care must be taken during installation to ensure that moisture can't get in under the surface; if it does, the natural fiber backing will rot and the floor will have to be replaced. Linoleum is also warm underfoot and acoustically gentle, a plus for anyone who despairs of the clattering echoes produced in rooms lined with hard surfaces. It's also a naturally anti-bacterial surface, hence its regular appearances in hospitals, where hygiene is a priority. Modern linoleum comes in hundreds of base colors and patterns; various decorative insets and border strips are also available.

Like linoleum, cork is an agreeably organic product that is soft and warm to the touch. Cork tiles are made by mixing granulated cork with either natural or synthetic binders, then baking. Natural cork tiles are also available bleached or tinted in a variety of pastel shades. The tiles are sealed in situ and should be sanded back and refinished every three or four years.

Rubber is another natural product choice, being made from the sap of the rubber tree mixed with a bonding ingredient, such as chalk, cork or powdered slate. Rubber comes in tile or sheet form and is available in the usual overwhelming variety of colors. Studded rubber is a particularly good choice in the kitchen, its slip-proof surface proving valuable in wet areas.

Vinyl, a synthetic material, has two great advantages. First, it is essentially a low-cost product, although some manufacturers produce a premium product with comparably higher prices. Second, it has the knack of imitating just about every other flooring surface, from parquetry to precious stone. In so doing, it makes it possible to employ those looks in cases where the authentic material is either too expensive or too difficult to install. It is very low maintenance, and with regular cleaning should last for decades without the hassle of resurfacing that accompanies wooden and sometimes stone floors.

HARD SURFACES
Ceramic tiles are a popular choice in the kitchen. Fully vitrified tiles and tiles with a matte glaze do not get slippery when wet and are therefore suitable for use in the kitchen. Unlike standard tiles, fully vitrified tiles are a solid color throughout, so small chips will not be glaringly obvious. Tiles are hardwearing and easy to maintain, but like all hard surfaces they will reflect sound, which could result in a noisy room.

Terra-cotta floors are composed of tiles of baked clay. They have a warm and earthy look, but are extremely porous and must be sealed for use in the kitchen. Some sealers darken the color of the natural tile.

❸

❶ Linoleum comes both in sheet form and in tiles. The tiled version must be installed by an experienced professional. If water is allowed to seep through imperfect joins, the natural fiber backing of the tiles may decay.

❷ Ceramic tiles make for a no-nonsense, hardwearing surface. They may, however, crack under excessive weight. Islands can be surprisingly heavy, especially when made with hardwood or surfaced with granite or concrete countertops. Before installing an island, check to see that its weight will not be too much for the tiles to bear.

❸ Cork is a classic floor choice in a family kitchen, being soft and warm underfoot, easy to maintain and install — and affordable, too.

Marble can be laid in tile or slab form. It is an inherently cold material, though underfloor heating can be installed to rectify that natural tendency. The color of marble ranges from whites and pale grays through roses to some quite dark greens, all with the characteristic veining. Marble tends to have a grand look, though it can be used subtly in a graceful country kitchen. It is porous and must be sealed to avoid stains.

Granite is another magnificent stone surface, ranging in color from beige to rusty red to near black with a characteristic strength and resilience that will probably never be tested in a domestic kitchen. Like marble, it is a naturally cold material that may require underfloor heating in a cold climate.

Terrazzo is a wonderful hybrid product that has something of the stature of a stone floor, but comes in a range of looks that embraces the warm, the whimsical, the classical and the bold. It is made by strewing an aggregate material through a concrete base. Conventionally, the concrete is mixed with marble chips, but the modern version offers a more interesting range of aggregates, including shell, colored glass and fragments of metals, such as brass or copper. The product can be further customized by adding tints to the concrete base. Terrazzo can be poured in situ, or laid as slabs or tiles.

Concrete is a product that has been reborn as a design material in recent years. Raw concrete slab floors, so common in modern homes, can be polished to a luminous, stylish and edgily sophisticated finish or overlaid with a tinted screed, then buffed and sealed. Giving a polished finish to a raw floor is a reasonably inexpensive treatment, but tinted screeds or those that incorporate decorative particles, terrazzo-style, can be more expensive. A concrete floor is naturally porous, so it must be appropriately sealed.

❶ Vinyls come in a variety of finishes, from solid colors to elaborate replicas of opulent marble or parquetry. Borders give a finished look to the kitchen floor, and can either be simple, like the contrast line shown here, or sophisticated, in the form of look-alike mosaic edging or classic Etruscan borders.

❶

❷ Many types of flooring possess the physical characteristics necessary for the hardworking life of a kitchen floor. Of all of them, however, wood is perhaps the only one that can be used right through the rest of the house. For that reason, it is very often applied in open-plan living areas, creating a seamless and consistent floor type throughout. ❷

WOOD

Like the soft surfaces, wood is a material that yields, making it comfortable to stand or walk on for long periods. Wood is easy to keep clean, but can be damaged by water so must be sealed properly. Oil finishes and synthetic finishes, such as polyurethane, will wear over time, and must be sanded back and reapplied every three or four years.

Tongue-and-groove floorboards are the most common installation method. Parquetry is an option, but the many intricate joins of the surface make it particularly susceptible to damage from water and heat. If it is well cared for, it can be used in the kitchen, but simple floorboards are probably a more reliable alternative.

Different species offer different hues and grains, from the rugged and knotty pine, through to the fine-grained dark brown of stained cherry or mahogany. Buying plantation wood ensures that the floorboards have not been fashioned from a threatened species or sourced from rapidly depleting rainforest resources.

Recycled or salvaged floorboards are products that have been retrieved from demolished buildings. They tend to have more character than new floorboards and sometimes come in extra-large widths that have been deemed infeasible to produce in modern mills. These can add charm to any room, but make a particularly sympathetic surface choice in a refurbished period home. The extra work involved in sourcing, removing, sorting and re-presenting recycled floorboards adds to their cost relative to brand new floorboards.

Remilled wooden beams are large, structural pieces, such as roof beams, that have been milled into conventional tongue-and-groove form. The chief advantage of these is that they can achieve unusually broad widths, up to 10 or 12 inches

❸

(25 or 30 cm) in some cases. Remilled beams are a rarer, more labor-intensive product and therefore tend to be even more expensive than recycled floorboards.

Way down the scale in terms of price is the plywood floor. Plywood is a material made from layers of pine, with the grain of each consecutive layer laid at right angles to the one before it. This structure gives the material great stability. Plywood comes in sheet form and can be screwed onto joists to achieve an unusually low-cost wooden floor. It can also be painted or treated with a stain. The disadvantage of plywood is that its surface is just the upper layer of a multitude of very thin veneers and can be damaged relatively easily. Like all wood, it must be sealed against water damage.

❶ Flagstone flooring enhances this modern kitchen's rustic air.

❷ In a poorly lit kitchen, a floor with an ultra glossy, highly reflective finish will make the most of whatever light is available. When wet, however, it becomes extremely slippery. For that reason it is probably not the best option in a household with very young or very old family members.

❸ High-gloss finishes on wooden floors can look spectacular, but they do show scratches and can be dangerous when wet. In a kitchen, it's best to opt for either a matte or semi-gloss finish.

COLORS

Nothing signals the personality of a space like color. A kitchen dressed in harvest yellow is cheerful and gregarious, while another clad in cool whites and ash grays is aloof and urbane. A lacquered, red feature wall declares Asian influences; an expanse of fuchsia pink recalls the languorous South Pacific. Quality comes at a cost for most kitchen fixtures, but the character-defining, space-creating power of color is yours for the price of a can of paint.

CHOOSING COLORS

The contemporary kitchen, whether or not it is incorporated into a multipurpose, open-plan living space, is very much exposed to the life of the house. For that reason, the colors used in the kitchen should really be considered in terms of the palette used throughout the house. Deviating from the dominant palette has the potential to be stimulating, but it more commonly reads as a disruption, an irregularity that gives the space an unwelcoming, makeshift atmosphere.

Whites and off-whites are by far the most popular color choices in the kitchen, and with good reason. They make the most of the available light, they tend to make rooms feel more spacious, they evoke attractive notions of cleanliness and they let the glorious hues of fresh produce give life to the space.

It's worth remembering at this point that a basically "white" room can be rendered in any one of an extraordinary range of tints. Most paint manufacturers offer dozens of different versions of white, some as many as two or three hundred. Sometimes the active tint in these colored whites is easily identifiable, such as the most preciously fragile of pale pinks or the very crispest and palest of pale greens. In other instances, however, the tint is scarcely discernible. These hues can be extremely valuable in balancing the cool or warm tendencies of the light in north- or south-facing rooms.

Employing pale neutrals, such as a bleached khaki or a gentle smoky gray, to nudge a shade more color into a room can add some personality to a kitchen without losing the space-creating, light-enhancing qualities of the whites and off-whites.

PREVIOUS PAGES A cool, monochromatic scheme achieves a sense of space in a modern interior with a compact floorplan, while a deep claret contributes a coziness to an open-plan kitchen in a sprawling family home.

 Colors are highly adaptable elements: depending on the context, they can be loud or hushed, dominant or subtle, vivid or delicate. Yellow, for example, can bestow a sunlit freshness on a kitchen when teamed with white and an abundance of natural light sources, while in partnership with dark wood and atmospheric feature lighting it imbues a space with a suave and sophisticated air.

 Knowing that you like red or blue or green is only a starting point. Use the color cues of the natural environment to refine your palette. Something as simple as a bowl of pomegranates or a tidepool of seashells could suggest a scheme of shades made up of coral, russet, rawhide and melon.

 Selecting colors that lie close together on the color wheel is a sure way of imbuing a space with calm, consistent confidence. Remember, though, that the colors should have a similar tone. Teaming a brilliant lime with a dull olive will yield an uneven, uncomfortable result, but a combination of muted shades, such as pea green, fir green, sea mist and khaki, will be a success.

 All-white color schemes are an appealing option for the kitchen, suggesting freshness and everlasting cleanliness. They can, however, tend toward the clinical and the impersonal. A move toward sandy, stony, beachy neutrals offers more ground for the creation of something uniquely personal. Those subtler shades also sit more comfortably with the natural surfaces so common in contemporary kitchens, such as wood, marble, limestone and granite.

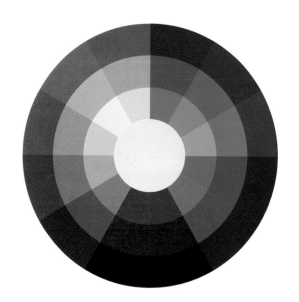

COLOR WHEEL The schoolbook connotations of the color wheel tend to daunt some people, yet it is invaluable as a starting point for creative color combinations. Pick out colors from around the wheel in analogous, complementary or complex combinations for schemes that are either subtle or dynamic. The best outcomes are achieved when all color choices lie within the same band of intensity.

Blue is another kitchen standard. Teamed with white, it recalls the tradition of willow-pattern tableware, establishing a timeless quality that also manages to look clean and fresh. It is also an excellent partner for most woods. Pine, beech, Oregon — any of the woods that have a yellow to orange tone — strike a handsome contrast with blue, a complementary color that lies on the opposite side of the color wheel.

Creams, yellows and terra cotta warm the kitchen with their glowing tones even when the sun isn't shining. Their earthy origins give them a natural connection with rooms that have a rustic look, whether they are influenced by the charm of a country kitchen or the sun-baked hospitality of the Mediterranean.

The rise of red as a fashion color for kitchens is linked to the increasing influence of Asian style. Like the yellows and terra cotta, red can bring a warm and welcoming look to a space, but the natural intensity of the hue can be overwhelming. Whether the kitchen is contained in a separate room or is part of an open-plan area, red is probably best limited to a feature wall or two.

❶

❶ Here, blushing cream cabinetry is a smooth partner for the pink-toned rock maple and brushbox hardwood of the floor and island.

❷ Kitchens designed to sit sympathetically within a period home benefit from the use of mellow tones. Here, pale mustard cabinetry implies a sense of age in keeping with the surrounding architectural environment.

❸ The popularity of blue isn't surprising given the way that it works with two common elements of the contemporary kitchen: wooden floors and stainless steel surfaces and appliances. Blue teams neatly with steel surfaces and strikes a confident contrast with most mid-brown woods. The tropical seas of the South Pacific were the color cue for this exotic marine shade.

❷

❸

COMBINING COLORS

If you find that the overwhelming possibilities of color combinations cloud your judgment and rob you of your instincts, then returning to the basics can be a worthwhile exercise. In technical terms, there are essentially four foolproof strategies.

The simplest of all is the monochrome color scheme. It's not quite as limiting as it sounds: rather than using a single hue on every wall, cushion, lampshade and tabletop, it's a matter of layering a number of shades throughout the space. Imagine a deliciously plump sofa with lavender-blue loose covers scattered with serge and navy blue cushions in a room where the walls are painted a delicate ice blue. Even with such variations in tone, a monochromatic scheme can be somewhat under-stimulating. Prints, patterns and textured finishes can save the simple scheme from lapsing into dullness.

Slightly more sophisticated is the analogous color scheme, utilizing three or four shades that lie alongside each other on the color wheel. The variations between these shades can be quite minimal, but for the sake of illustrating the point, think of a scheme that includes yellow, lime and green, or green, turquoise and blue. These combinations work because all colors in the series are the same "temperature" — being either warm colors or cool colors — and because they all share one underlying hue. In the case of the first example, yellow is the constant; in the second example, it is blue. These strong connections ensure a sense of harmony.

❶

① When designing a color scheme, don't forget that such elements as glass, wood and steel also figure in the palette. Most domestic woods tend to have either yellow or orange tones. Blue and blue-green, colors that lie opposite those hues on the color wheel, offer the most dramatic contrast. A kitchen that juxtaposes blue surfaces with wood will not disappear into the background.

② Cool blues and purples are easy partners for the stainless steel surfaces of this very modern kitchen.

③ Shades such as terra cotta, ocher and umber resonate with the natural tones of the most common wood varieties. Here, the unity achieved by the use of those warm hues gives this kitchen a surprisingly low profile, despite the visual punch of the earth-red feature wall.

② ③

If you're looking for more dynamism in a color scheme, consider the complementary combinations. These are made up of colors that lie directly opposite each other on the color wheel, such as navy and burnt umber, fuchsia pink and bud green, or eggplant and chartreuse. These pairings have instant appeal, but remember that they are naturally stimulating; if you want your kitchen to sit inconspicuously in an open-plan area, complementary combinations are best avoided.

Complex combinations deal with colors located at equal intervals around the color wheel. Complex trios include terra cotta, chartreuse and lavender, or saffron, turquoise and plum. A complex quartet might be rose pink, leaf green, lavender and butternut. Using so many colors can result in a scheme of satisfying depth and diversity, but it does require deft handling and so is best left to experienced decorators.

Whichever approach you choose, allow one color to dominate. When colors are equally prominent, they tend to vie for attention, keeping the eye flicking from one surface to the next and undermining any sense of composure. Instead, stagger the proportions, letting one color take the lead and another perform a supporting role. Additional colors should then appear as accents.

① Color can be influential in the success of an open-plan area, distinguishing between zones or unifying them as required. In this small house, a consistent palette throughout the kitchen, living and dining spaces serves to make the entire area feel as large as possible.

② Blue and white is a classic color combination, particularly in the kitchen. Always fresh, always cool and very easy to embellish with either modern accessories or antique china, it is an excellent choice for anyone just beginning to work with color.

③ Bright colors in dynamic combination can be a sensible option for young families. The inherent vitality of such schemes seems to swallow up the inevitable scattering of toys, schoolbags and abandoned items of clothing. In this kitchen, aqua and tangerine do the job.

②

③

SHAPES

The prospect of designing a kitchen floorplan might seem
intimidating at first, but really it's an exercise in simple problem
solving. Most of the big decisions — where to position the range
or the sink, how to configure the storage, where to install the work
surfaces — are answered by logic. Just pay heed to the dimensions
of the room and the limits of the budget and proceed accordingly.

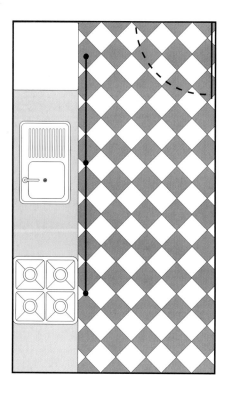

PREVIOUS PAGES The structures of galley and U-shaped kitchens produce a natural perimeter that contains and protects the work space of an open-plan kitchen.

❶ Locating the refrigerator close to the door means that a cook can get on with the business of cooking in a single-wall kitchen without interruption from other household members dropping by for drinks or snacks. Make sure, however, that the two doors do not obstruct each other when open.

❷ The counter between the sink and the cooktop will become the primary work surface. If there's money to be spent on a quality counter, spend it here.

❸ In an open-plan situation, dining tables can supplement the limited work surfaces of the single-wall kitchen.

ONE-WALL KITCHENS

A small, narrow room — even one with little more than 60 to 70 square feet (5.5 to 6.5 sq m) in floor area — can make an effective kitchen provided it is well planned. The emphasis, of course, is on spatial efficiency, but some of the design issues vary according to the structure of the space and the number of people using it on a regular basis.

FLOORPLAN

There's very little you can do to vary the floorplan of a one-wall kitchen. In order to include a cooktop, a sink and some counter space for food preparation, you will need a length of at least 10 feet (3 m). A width of 6 feet (1.8 m) is the bare minimum required to accommodate 24-inch (61-cm) counters and some floorspace for cooks.

The conventional wisdom is that the longest expanse of clear counter space should run between the cooktop and the sink. Locating the cooktop at the far end and the sink, refrigerator and perhaps a microwave oven at the end closer to the door means that a second person can access a cup of coffee or a snack while the cook prepares a meal.

EQUIPMENT

Take a realistic look at your cooking habits. Do you use the cooktop frequently for stir fries, grills and stews, but rarely get around to baking in the oven? Do you do very little home cooking at all, preferring instead to grab take-out on the way home from work and eat out in restaurants over the weekend? Despite its prevalence, the standard oven-cooktop-microwave oven set-up of the average kitchen is not compulsory. Perhaps your needs could be met by a cooktop alone, in which case an oven would only take up valuable space in a small kitchen.

If you were to concede that all your cooking was done in a microwave oven, you would not be the first person to omit the conventional cooktop and oven from your kitchen: developers have been designing pared-back, range-free kitchens in city apartment blocks for the best part of a decade.

Forgoing a full-size refrigerator in favor of a half-height bar fridge or an under-counter refrigerator drawer may be a way of freeing up more space. Similarly, half-width dishwashers and dishwasher drawers cater for those who don't need the capacity of a full-size dishwasher.

Taking stock of what you need and fitting your kitchen accordingly can liberate the floorplan, reducing the space and volume spent on equipment and thereby increasing the floor and wall area available to other elements, such as storage or a compact dining area. It may even reduce your consumption of energy and water, saving you money and preserving the Earth's limited resources at the same time. Remember, though, that if it is too unconventional, your personalized kitchen may have a negative effect on the resale value of the property.

STORAGE

Wall-mounted cabinets provide valuable storage space, but can make a narrow kitchen feel very claustrophobic. If they are essential, opt for glass-fronted cabinets that foster a sense of depth. Clear glass will let you see all the way through to the back wall, but even frosted glass has a translucency that alleviates the sense of enclosure. If you decide to use wall-mounted cabinets, don't then waste the space between the top of the upper cabinets and the ceiling. Instead, install an additional row of cabinets or a series of shelves, or have extra-tall wall cabinets custom made so that all the space is utilized.

❷

❸

Favor drawers over cabinets below the counter. Stepping to one side to open a drawer and view its contents is spatially more efficient than the process of stepping back to open the cabinet doors before crouching down and peering inside. Full-height, pull-out pantries are particularly useful in a one-wall kitchen. Fit them at the far end of the room, and they can even be left open while meals are being prepared, making every item visible and accessible without impeding the cook's path around the kitchen. With sliding doors on wall-mounted cabinets, a cabinet can be left open while the kitchen is in use without fear of its door connecting with anyone's head.

Don't forget vertical space when looking to increase storage capacity. Even the gap between upper and lower cabinets can be fitted with slim shelves or a hanging rail system.

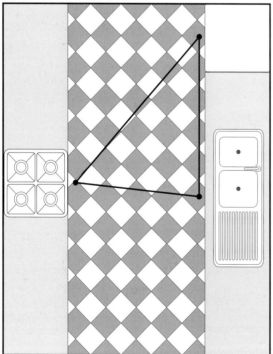

❶
❷   WORK SURFACES

One-wall kitchens can be used comfortably by a single cook, but begin to reveal their shortcomings once a second cook enters the frame. Lack of counter space is the main problem. Pull-out counters installed directly below the fitted counter are one way of introducing extra work surfaces. Some sinks feature accessories that cover the basin, converting it into useful counter space when the sink itself is not in use. Small trolleys or wheel-mounted islands that can be pushed into a corner or into another room entirely are also valuable and can offer extra storage capacity as well.

GALLEY KITCHENS

Galley kitchens make the most of a small room, but function so efficiently that they are often employed in situations where space is not an issue, for example in an open-plan living area.

③

FLOORPLAN

Just like the classic ship's galley, the domestic galley kitchen comprises two banks of cabinetry on opposing walls. The corridor between them should be at least 4 feet (1.2 m) wide; any less, and access to the lower cabinets will prove difficult. An extra-wide corridor should be avoided, because it will only increase the distance between appliances on either side of the room, undermining the set-up's inherent spatial economy.

It is possible to squeeze a galley kitchen into a particularly narrow room by installing 18-inch (45-cm) counters, rather than the normal 24-inch (61-cm) ones, along one wall. The narrower cabinets will not accommodate a conventional sink, dishwasher, refrigerator, cooktop or oven, but the area could house small appliances, such as blenders and toasters.

① Full-height cabinets at either end of a single-wall kitchen form a pleasant, rather sculptural frame for the work space in this diminutive open-plan area.

② In a galley kitchen, positioning the cooktop and sink on opposite walls maximizes the amount of counter space available to both. It makes sense in this case to site the cooktop on the exterior wall. This is because the installation of the necessary ventilation unit can be both costly and unsightly if ducting has to run across the room to the far counter and then drop down from the ceiling to sit above the burners.

③ A raised backsplash on the outer counter of a galley kitchen in an open-plan situation shields the mess of the work surface from the living areas.

Assuming the conventional twin banks of 24-inch (61-cm) cabinetry are in place, the next step in the design process is to decide on the locations of the three primary work sites — cooktop, sink and refrigerator. The refrigerator is best located close to the door so that it can be accessed by any family member without interruption to the cook's work in the main body of the kitchen. In most cases, both the sink and the cooktop — with its necessary partner, the ventilation unit — are positioned on an exterior wall to simplify and therefore economize on the installation of water pipes and ducting. Such a structure also makes it possible for the stretch of counter space between those two work sites to be illuminated by natural light entering through a series of windows. Ideally, the floorplan would allow for useful work surfaces on both sides of the cooktop, but if it must be positioned close to one end of the cabinetry, leave at least 18 inches (45 cm) between it and the wall to make room for saucepan handles and swinging elbows. An alternative is to locate cooktop and sink opposite each other on parallel walls. This set-up maximizes counter space at each site while maintaining a comfortably small walking distance between the two.

Galley kitchens are often employed in open-plan areas, in which case the second wall of cabinetry really takes the form of a long island or peninsula. It's an excellent choice in the circumstances, with the outer run of cabinetry forming a natural boundary between the kitchen and the living spaces, providing the discipline and definition that is often lacking in open-plan areas. For comparatively little additional outlay, a breakfast bar can be attached to the far side of the outer cabinetry, creating an informal eating area and a perch for kitchen onlookers.

Cabinets can be suspended from the ceiling to provide an open-plan galley kitchen with extra storage space. Open shelves or glass-doored cabinets will maintain the lightweight look of open-plan areas.

STORAGE

Like the one-wall kitchen, the galley kitchen runs the risk of feeling uncomfortably cramped if lined on both sides by not just base cabinets but wall-mounted cabinets as well. Glass-fronted wall cabinets will reduce that sensation of enclosure.

Wall cabinets come in standard depths of either 18 inches (45 cm) or 24 inches (61 cm). Using the deeper cabinets at the ends and the narrower ones in the middle contributes some shape and movement to an otherwise fairly rigid space. Using angled or curved cabinets to mark the shift in depth will result in a more fluid look.

Full-height cabinets, such as pull-out pantries or units that incorporate fitted wall ovens, should be located next to an end wall to minimize their visual impact.

❶ The interior wall of cabinetry extends beyond the work space of this open galley kitchen and into the living areas. The effect is to unify the look of the whole room and to supply storage space for books, games, audiovisual equipment and the like.

❷ Locating the cooktop on the interior wall of the open-plan galley ensures that the hottest, messiest and noisiest business of the kitchen is kept at a distance from the recreational areas. A simple table can be used as a work surface, or as a place to sit down with a cup of coffee mid-morning.

WORK SURFACES

One thing that the galley kitchen has in abundance — relative to floor area, at least — is counter space. If space allows, think about installing multiple work surfaces, thereby creating multiple workstations so that two or more people can use the kitchen at the same time for different purposes. A primary food-preparation surface around the cooktop is essential, but other possibilities are a breakfast area fitted with power outlets for coffee maker and toaster or a pastry-making counter near the oven, set at the lower 30-inch (76-cm) height that is preferable for weight-bearing tasks, such as kneading and rolling.

L-SHAPED KITCHENS

The L-shaped kitchen is a neat and effective solution in a small, narrow room, while its openness allows space for a friendly table setting in larger rooms. It is not the best option for an open-plan area, because it fully exposes the work of the kitchen to the living areas, meaning that harried meal preparation and post-feast dirty dishes will always be on show.

FLOORPLAN

The angle of the L-shaped kitchen is naturally conducive to the provision of an efficient work triangle between the cooktop, the refrigerator and the sink. The cooktop and the sink are usually best sited on exterior walls to allow easy access for plumbing and ducting. The exterior wall location also means that the main work surface, which conventionally runs between the sink and the cooktop, is likely to benefit from whatever natural light is available.

As for most kitchens, positioning the refrigerator near the door and away from the main cooking area makes it easy for

❶ The structure of an L-shaped kitchen lends itself quite naturally to a compact and comfortable work triangle. Where possible, the counter space between the sink and the cooktop should be maximized, as this is likely to become the main work surface.

❶

❷ A large kitchen, such as this one in a rambling country house, leaves plenty of room for a dining table. Such a table will inevitably be used as a place for food preparation — even when, as in this case, there are ample work surfaces within the kitchen cabinetry. For that reason, the table should be made of a robust material such as wood.

❷

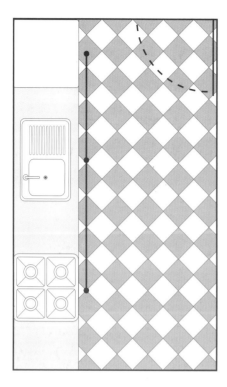

members of the household to drop in for a cool drink or a bite to eat without disturbing the cook's work. For the same reason, it can be advantageous to site the microwave oven and perhaps even an appliance garage in this area. Doing so creates a second workstation that is independent of the primary work triangle. Such a structure can have an enormous impact on the smooth functioning of a family kitchen.

The inner corner of the L-shape can prove an awkward location for storage. An alternative approach is to square off the angle and site the cooktop and oven here. The twin work surfaces provided by countertops on either side of the cooktop are a cook's dream. If the oven is located elsewhere, the space below the cooktop can be fitted with deep drawers for pot storage. This kind of arrangement tends to become a focal point in an L-shaped kitchen, so it can be an excellent place to show off a good-looking, high-performance range.

The L-shaped kitchen is the classic format for an eat-in kitchen in a small house or apartment. As long as appliances are sensibly located, the main meal-preparation area and the dining area will occupy diagonally opposite corners of the room, meaning that the table can comfortably be used by one person for non-cooking activities such as school homework or bill paying while another gets on with the business of cooking.

STORAGE

The internal angle of the L-shaped kitchen poses particular challenges for storage. Installing two banks of drawers on the adjacent walls is a clumsy solution. A single, L-shaped cabinet is likewise an unappealing option, creating a bay of storage that is dark and difficult to access. Rotating shelves hidden behind cupboard doors can work in this situation, as can open shelving. Use shelves that are narrower than the base units so that the back of the corner shelf is not impossible to reach.

❶ Positioning the cooktop and the sink on adjacent walls tends to make the most of the available counter space. Installation can become expensive, however, if one of those walls is an internal wall. In such a case, the cost benefits of installing both units on the same external wall could be impossible to overlook. As long as there is a reasonable amount of counter space between the two, the kitchen should function quite efficiently.

❷ The peninsula of this U-shaped kitchen has been designed as a seating area.

❸ In this instance, the peninsula has been faced with simple, open shelves that serve the living areas.

WORK SURFACES

The structure of the L-shaped kitchen creates an "empty" corner that can be utilized for extra counter space. If the room is small, a folding table or even a long, drop-down countertop with multiple struts to support its length can be called into use as extra work surface when required and can also serve as an informal eating area. In larger rooms, the temptation to install a table and chairs will be hard to resist. The table can be used as an extra work space at any time, provided it has a robust surface. Remember, though, that tables are lower than conventional base cabinets and can become uncomfortable when used over extended periods for such tasks as chopping and mixing.

Bear in mind that the counter space between the cooktop and the sink tends to become the main food-preparation surface. If working with a tight budget, consider installing a high-performance material, such as stainless steel or granite, in this area while using less expensive materials, such as laminate, for the remaining work surfaces.

U-SHAPED KITCHENS

The U-shaped kitchen maximizes storage and counter space in large or small rooms. It's also common in open-plan situations where one of the two parallel sides takes the form of a peninsula, which extends out from a wall and marks the boundary between kitchen and living spaces.

FLOORPLAN

With so much space to play with, the most common mistake in the design of a U-shaped kitchen is a loose arrangement of appliances. No matter how generous the proportions of the

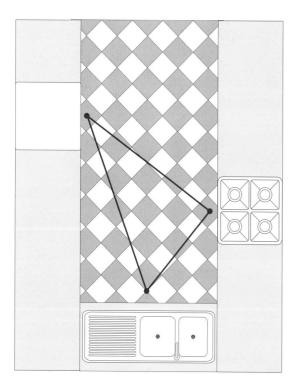

room, the temptation to space out the cooktop, refrigerator and sink should be avoided. It might seem that you're simply allowing more work surfaces around each of the major work centers, but in so doing you will create an inefficient work triangle that requires the cook to walk unnecessarily long distances during meal preparation. The convention is to limit the distance between each of those sites to 7 to 8 feet (2.1 to 2.4 m). An extra foot (30 cm) or so may not seem like much, but multiplied by the many trips taken between refrigerator and cooktop, cooktop and sink, and sink and refrigerator during the preparation of a single meal, it can add up to a considerable increase in distance travelled and can make the room uncomfortable to use.

The most sensible approach is to install both the sink and the cooktop toward the center of a run of cabinetry, allowing plenty of work space on either side. Whether on adjacent or opposite walls, the distance between the cooktop and the sink should not exceed 7 to 8 feet (2.1 to 2.4 m) if possible. The refrigerator should be located at the end of a run of cabinetry, close to the entrance to the kitchen. Thus positioned, the sink and cooktop compose a central work core which can be used without interruption from any member of the household stopping by the refrigerator for a drink or a snack.

The two awkward inner corners of the U-shape can become wasted spaces. One solution sometimes applied in L-shaped kitchens is to square off a corner and install a cooktop and oven there, the counters to either side presenting a handsome abundance of work space. Butterfly-wing double sinks are specifically designed for installation in corners and offer another opportunity for maximizing those problematic areas. Avoid installing the dishwasher at the internal end of a run of cabinetry, as it will obstruct the cabinets on the adjacent wall when open.

❶ In a U-shaped kitchen, sink and cooktop can be located on the same wall, on adjacent walls or on opposite walls; the size of the room, the ease of installation and the scope of the budget may restrict those choices. In any case, positioning the refrigerator close to the door will ensure that the work going on between those two main sites is not regularly interrupted by other household members.

❷ In this kitchen, the inherently generous storage capacity has been supplemented by glass-fronted units for table linen and glass-ware, spice drawers and wine storage.

EQUIPMENT

The extra capacity afforded by the format of the U-shaped kitchen makes the appliance garage an entirely justifiable inclusion. Located along with the refrigerator somewhere close to the entrance of the kitchen, an appliance garage fitted with coffee maker, toaster and even a microwave oven becomes an independent workstation, accessible to anyone who just wants to drop in and grab a casual meal.

STORAGE

The internal angles of the U-shaped kitchen make for deep, dark cabinets where items stored at the rear are easily lost and forgotten. Rotating shelves located behind cabinet doors reduce the problem; shelves with guard rails ensure that small items don't slip off when the unit is in motion. Fixed, open shelving can also provide a solution, as long as the shelves are narrower than the depth of the surrounding base cabinets. Any items stashed at the back of corner shelves measuring 24 inches (61 cm) deep — whether or not they are faced by cabinet doors — will prove almost impossible to access.

In open-plan kitchens, one of the two parallel sides of the U-shape takes the form of a peninsula. The usefulness of this counter can be maximized by installing back-to-back cabinetry. If floorspace is in good supply, you might consider an extra-deep counter with 24-inch (61-cm) cabinets serving the kitchen and 18-inch (45-cm) deep cabinets providing storage space for tableware and table linen close to the dining table. Even a bank of 6-inch or 8-inch (15-cm or 20-cm) cabinets could be used to store drinking glasses.

WORK SURFACES

The peninsula of a U-shaped kitchen in an open-plan area can extend beyond the kitchen into the living area. The extended

counter increases the area available for food preparation and the overhang, when provided with stools for seating, can be used as a breakfast bar.

It's reasonably easy to accommodate a work island in a large U-shaped kitchen. If the island is on wheels, it can be pulled into service wherever it is needed most: to supplement the work surfaces around a cooktop, to provide more clean-up area around the sink after a big dinner party or to serve as a separate work surface close to the refrigerator when other family members are putting together a simple snack. A more substantial, fixed island can do triple service as work surface, storage unit and informal eating area. Remember to position the overhang of the counter in such a way that stools are located away from the activity centers of cooktop and sink.

INDEX

CREDITS

1 Architect: Daryl Le Grew; Kitchen designer: Jos van Bree, Domus Kitchens; Photographer: Peter Hyatt

2–3 Architect: Dale Mulfinger and Tim Fuller, SALA Architects; Interior designer: Talla Skogmo, Gunkelman Interior Design; Photographer: Tim Maloney

4–5 Designer: Chris Ralston; Photographer: Anton Curley

6–7 Architect: Andrew Patterson, Patterson Co Partners Architects; Photographer: Bruce Nicholson

8–9 (Left) Architect: Chris Wilson, Wilson & Hill Architects; Photographer: Lloyd Park; (center) Designer: Kira Gray, Kitchens by Design; Photographer: Anton Curley; (right) Architect: Jane Sachs and Thomas Hut, Hut Sachs Studio; Interior designer: Joe D'Urso and Tom Flynn; Photographer: John Umberger

10–11 Top row (left) Architect: Bud Brannigan; Photographer: David Sandison; (center) Architect: Brian Quirk, Quirk & Albakri; Photographer: Peter Mealin; (right) Architect: Daryl Le Grew; Kitchen designer: Jos van Bree, Domus Kitchens; Photographer: Peter Hyatt. Middle row (left) Architect: Gerard Murtagh; Photographer: David Sandison; (center) Architect: James McCalligan, JMA Architects; Photographer: Tim Maloney; (right) Designer: Jane Agnew; Photographer: Robert Frith. Bottom row (left) Kitchen designer: Diana Meckfessel;

Photographer: Tim Maloney; (center) Andrew Patterson, Patterson Co Partners Architects; Photographer: Bruce Nicholson; (right) Designer: Milvia Hannah, International Interiors; Photographer: Paul McCredie

12–13 (1) Designer: Cheryl Kees, In Detail; Interior designer: Nancy Woodcock Greenfield, Greenfield Galleries; Photographer: Gary Langhammer; (2) Architect: Gerard Lynch, Kevin Hayes Architects; Photographer: David Sandison

14–15 (1) Designer: Jane Agnew; Photographer: Robert Frith; (2) Designer: Shirley McFarlane, Kitchensmith Inc; Photographer: John Umberger; (3) Architect: Julia Stainback; Interior designer: Libby Patrick; Kitchen Designer: Matthew D. Rao; Photographer: John Umberger

16–17 Architect: Darren Jessop, Jessop Townsend; Photographer: Anton Curley

18–19 (1) Architect: Nicholas Stevens; Photography: Claude Lapeyre; (2) Designer: Mark White, Kitchen Encounters, assisted by Craig Heinrich; Photographer: Keel Harris; (3) Designer: Linda Christensen, Kitchens by Design; Architectural designer: Peter Diprose; Photographer: Anton Curley

20–23 Architect: Bud Brannigan; Photographer: David Sandison

24–25 Architect: Michael Folk, Folk & Lichtman; Photographer: Simon Kenny

26–31 Architect: André Hodgskin Architects; Photographer: Anton Curley

32–35 Architect: Paul Uhlmann; Photographer: David Sandison

36–39 Architect: David Swan Interior Design; Photographer: Michael Nicholson

40–41 Architect: Michael & Michael Design; Photographer: David Sandison

42–45 Architect: John Chaplin; Kitchen designer: Ingrid Geldof; Photographer: Doc Ross

46–47 Architect: Sheppard & Rout; Photographer: Lloyd Park

48–51 Architect: Cook, Sargisson & Pirie; Photographer: Bruce Nicholson

52–57 Architect: Karl Romandi, Karl Romandi & Helen DeLuis Architects; Photographer: Simon Kenny

58–61 Architect: James McCalligan, JMA Architects; Photographer: Tim Maloney

62–63 Designer: Hardy Interiors; Photographer: Simon Kenny

64–67 Architect: Jonathan Waddy Architects; Photographer: Paul McCredie

68–69 Architect: Dorothy Street, Kitchen Living; Photographer: Lloyd Park

70–73 Architect: Diana Meckfessel; Photographer: Tim Maloney

74–75 Architect: Sam Wells and Diana L. Marley, Sam Wells and Associates; Photographer: Tim Maloney

76–81 Architect: Chris Ralston; Photographer: Anton Curley

82–85 Hedgpeth Architects; Photographer: Tim Maloney

86–89 Kitchen designer: Sally Holland and Tony Parker; Photographer: Anton Curley

90–93 Architect: Brian Quirk, Quirk & Albakri; Photographer: Peter Mealin

94–97 Architect: Leon House, Leon House Design; Photographer: Robert Frith

98–99 Architect: Michael Banney, m3architecture; Photographer: David Sandison

100–101 Architect: Robyn Labb, Kitchens by Design; Photographer: Bruce Nicholson

102–107 Architect: Athfield Architects; Photographer: Paul McCredie

108–109 Designer: Darryl Gordon Design; Photographer: Simon Kenny

110–113 Architect: Darren Jessop, Jessop Townsend Architects; Photographer: Bruce Nicholson

114–117 Architect: John Mills Architects; Photographer: Paul McCredie

118–119 Architect: Jane Sachs and Thomas Hut, Hut Sachs Studio; Photographer: John Umberger

120–123 Architect: Lindy Small Architecture; Photographer: Tim Maloney

124–125 Architect: Chris Wilson, Wilson & Hill Architects; Photographer: Lloyd Park

126–129 Kitchen designer: Kitchens by Design; Photographer: Gérald Lopez

130–131 Architect: Linda Christensen, Kitchens by Design; Photographer: Anton Curley

132–133 Architect: Philip Follent, Philip Follent Architects; Photographer: David Sandison

134–137 Architect: Kerry Mason, Architecture Warren & Maloney; Photographer: Lloyd Park

138–139 Architect: Gabriel & Elizabeth Poole Design; Photographer: David Sandison

140–143 Architect: Linda Christensen, Kitchens by Design; Photographer: Bruce Nicholson

144–145 Architect: Gerard Murtagh; Photographer: David Sandison

146–147 Designer: Fay Bresolin; Photographer: Paul McCredie

148–149 Architect: Paul Clarke, Crosson Clarke Architects; Photographer: Bruce Nicholson

150–151 Architect: BBP Architects; Photographer: Shania Shegedyn

152–153 Architect: Grant Amon; Photographer: Shania Shegedyn

154–159 Architect: Richard Wolfgramm; Photographer: Tim Maloney

160–163 Architect: Veryan Del Moro, Italy and Kitchens; Photographer: Anton Curley

164–165 Architect: Jeff Tan, Unique Kitchen Fusion; Photographer: Peter Mealin

166–167 Architect: Creazioni Kitchens; Photographer: Anton Curley

168–171 Architect: Mark Domiteaux, Domiteaux and Howard Architects; Photographer: Tim Maloney

172–173 Consultant: Jeff Tan, Unique Kitchen Fusion; Photographer: Peter Mealin

174–177 Designer: Jos van Bree, Domus Kitchens; Photographer: Peter Hyatt

178–179 Designer: Milvia Hannah, International Interiors; Photographer: Paul McCredie

180–181 Architect: Dorothy Street, Kitchen Living; Photographer: Lloyd Park

182–183 Architect: Mark Fosner, Moon Bros Inc.; Photographer: Tim Maloney

184–185 Architect: Julian Guthrie, Godward Guthrie Architecture; Photographer: Bruce Nicholson

186–189 Designer: Tony Cardamone, Cardamone Design; Photographer: Shania Shegedyn

190–193 Designer: Creazioni Kitchens and Shami Griffen; Photographer: Gérald Lopez

194–195 Architect: Keith Capell; Photographer: Simon Kenny

196–197 Designer: Suying Design Pte Ltd; Photographer: Tim Nolan

198–201 Architect: Sharon Cross Interior Design; Photographer: Anton Curley

202–203 (left) Architect: Veryan Del Moro, Italy and Kitchens; Photographer: Anton Curley; (right) Designer: Cheng Designs; Photographer: Matthew Millman

204–205 Architect: Richard Priest Architects; Photographer: Anton Curley

206–207 (1) Architect: BBP Architects; Photographer: Shania Shegedyn; (2) Architect: Shelly Gane, Cook Sargisson & Pirie; Photographer: Bruce Nicholson

208–209 (1) Architect: Diana Meckfessel; Photographer: Tim Maloney; (2) Architect: Crofton Umbers Design; Photographer: Anton Curley

210–211 (1) Image supplied by Neff Kitchen Manufacturers; (2) Architect: Paul Clarke, Crosson Clarke Architects; Photographer: Bruce Nicholson

212–213 (1) Designer: Sandra Grummitt; Photographer: Chris Parker; (2) Designer: Kira Gray, Kitchens by Design; Photographer: Anton Curley

214–215 Architect: David Kingwill; Photographer: Tim Maloney

216–217 (1) Architect: Jonathan Waddy Architects; Photographer: Paul McCredie; (2) Designer: Compleat Design; Photographer: Gérald Lopez; (3) Designer: Creazioni Kitchens and Shami Griffen; Photographer: Gérald Lopez; (4) Architect: Lindy Small Architecture; Photographer: Tim Maloney; (5) Architect: John Chaplin; Kitchen Designer: Ingrid Geldof Design; Photographer: Doc Ross

218–219 (1) Designer: Creazioni Kitchens; Photographer: Anton Curley; (2) Architect: Campbell, Luscombe Associates; Photographer: Simon Kenny

220–221 (1) Architect: Glen Johns, Henry Brown Kitchens; Photography courtesy of Henry Brown Kitchens; (2) Designer: Julius Blum; Photography courtesy of Julius Blum; (3) Architect: Chris Wilson, Wilson & Hill Architects;

Photographer: Lloyd Park; (4) Image supplied by Fisher & Paykel

222–223 (1) Designer: Creazioni Kitchens and Shami Griffen; Photographer: Gérald Lopez; Kitchen designer: Kay Charlton, Compleat Design; Architect: Mal Bartleet; Photographer: Gérald Lopez

224–225 (1) Architect: John Chaplin; Designer: Ingrid Geldof Design; Photographer: Doc Ross; Designer: Cameron Kimber; Photographer: Simon Kenny

226–227 (1) Designer: Milvia Hannah, International Interiors; Photographer: Paul McCredie; (2) Architect: Campbell, Luscombe Associates; Photographer: Simon Kenny; (2) Designer: Clive Champion; Photographer: Shania Shegedyn

228–229 (1) Architect: Lindy Leuschke, Leuschke Group Architects; Photographer: Bruce Nicholson; (2) Designer: Genesi; Photography courtesy of Genesi

230–231 (1) Designer: Kitchens by Design; Photographer: Gérald Lopez; (2) Designer: Jere M Bowden; Interior designer: Jay Miner, Miner Designs; Photographer: Tim Maloney

232–233 (1) Design: Carlsson Design; Photo courtesy of Carlsson Design; (2) Architect: Architecture Warren & Maloney; Photographer: Anton Curley

234–235 (1) Designer: Jennie Dunlop, Dunlop Design; Photographer: Bruce Nicholson; (2) Architect: Moon Bros; Photographer: John Umberger

236–237 Designer: Cheryl Kees, In Detail; Photographer: Gary Langhammer

238–239 (1) Architect: Malcolm Taylor, Xsite Architecture; Photographer: Bruce Nicholson; (2) Architect: Richard Priest Architects; Photographer: Anton Curley; (3) Architect: Tom Zurowski, Eastlake Studio; Photographer: Tim Maloney

240–241 (1) Architect: Darryl Gordon Design; Photographer: Simon Kenny; (2) Architect: Dale Mulfinger and Tim Fuller, SALA Architects; Photographer: Tim Maloney; (3) Designer: Steven J. Livingston, Studio Snaidero; Photographer: Tim Maloney

242–243 (1) Image supplied by Kitchen Workshop; Photographer: Peter Beattie; (2) Designer: Compleat Design; Photographer: Gérald Lopez; (3) Architect: Robert Blair in association with McLaughlin & Associates Building Consultants; Photographer: Shania Shegedyn

244–245 (1) Architect: Banham Architects; Photographer: Robert Frith; (2) Architect: André Hodgskin Architects; Photographer: Anton Curley; (3) Architect: Michael Banney, m3architecture; Photographer: David Sandison

246–247 (left) Architect: Brian Quirk, Quirk and Albakri; Photographer: Peter Mealin; (right) Architect: Lindy Small Architecture; Photographer: Tim Maloney

248–249 (1) Designer: Selina Tay, Collective Designs; Photographer: Peter Mealin; (2) Architect: Richard Wolgramm; Photographer: Tim Maloney; (3) Designer: Dorothy Street, Kitchen Living; Photographer: Lloyd Park; (4) Designer: Sharon Cross Interior Design; Photographer: Anton Curley;

(5) Architect: Darren Jessop, Jessop Townsend; Photographer: Anton Curley

250–251 (1) Designer: Terri Tan, Designworx Interior Consultant; Photographer: Tim Nolan; (2) Architect: Mulena Architects; Photographer: Anton Curley; (3) Designer: Sue Gillbanks; Photographer: Anton Curley

252–253 Designer: Alno; Photo courtesy of Alno

254–255 (1) Architect: Richard Priest Architects; Photographer: Anton Curley; (2) Architect: John Brooks; Photographer: Tim Maloney; (3) Designer: Sandra Grummitt; Photographer: Anton Curley

256–257 (1) Designer: Suying Design Pte Ltd; Photographer: Tim Nolan; (2) Architect: Keith Capell; Photographer: Simon Kenny; (3) Designer: Jere M. Bowden (Rutt of Atlanta); Photographer: Tim Maloney

258–259 Architect: Pat Jeffares; Photographer: Kallan MacLeod

260–261 (1) Architect: David Kingwill; Photographer: Tim Maloney; (2) Designer: Michael O'Brien, de Giulio Kitchen Design; Photographer: John Miller; (3) Designer: Chris Ralston; Photographer: Anton Curley

262–263 (1) Designer: Shirley McFarlane, Kitchensmith; Photographer: Thomas Birdwell; (2) Designer: Leon House, Leon House Design; Photographer: Robert Frith; (3) Architect: Jackson Clements Burrows; Photographer: Shania Shegedyn

264–265 Designer: Jane Agnew; Photographer: Robert Frith

266–267 (1) Architect: Patterson Co Partners Architects; Photographer: Bruce Nicholson; (2) Designer: Sue Gillbanks; Photographer: Anton Curley; (3) Designer: Jennie Dunlop, Dunlop Design; Photographer: Bruce Nicholson

268–269 (left) Designer: Linda Christensen, Kitchens by Design; Photographer: Bruce Nicholson; (right) Architect: John Mills Architects; Photographer: Paul McCredie

270–271 (1) Architect: Sam Wells and Diana L. Marley, Sam Wells and Associates; Photographer: Tim Maloney; (2) Designer: Kay Charlton, Compleat Design; Photographer: Gérald Lopez; (3) Architect: Sheppard & Rout; Photographer: Lloyd Park; (4) Architect: Jessop Townsend Architects; Photographer: Bruce Nicholson

272–273 (1) Designer: Steven J. Livingston, Studio Snaidero; Photographer: Tim Maloney; (2) Designer: Hardy Interiors; Photographer: Peter Bateman; (3) Designer: Robert Chapman; Photographer: Anton Curley; (4) Designer: Michelle Somerville; Photographer: Anton Curley; (5) Architect: Grant Amon; Photographer: Shania Shegedyn

274–275 (1) Kitchen designer: Diana Meckfessel; Photographer: Tim Maloney; (2) Architect: James McCalligan, JMA Architects; Photographer: Tim Maloney

276–277 (1) Designer: Terri Tan, Designworx Interior Consultant; Photographer: Tim Nolan; (2) Architect: Grant Amon; Photographer: Shania Shegedyn;

(3) Designer: Dorothy Street, Kitchen Living; Photographer: Lloyd Park

278–279 (1) Designer: Clive Champion; Photographer: Shania Shegedyn; (2) Architect: Karl Romandi, Karl Romandi & Helen DeLuis Architects; Designer: Michael Jan, Jan & Manton Design Architecture; Photographer: Simon Kenny

280–281 (1) Designer: Stefan Mayer, Scullery & Holz; Photographer: Simon Kenny; (2) Designer: Sharon Cross Interior Design; Photographer: Anton Curley; (3) Designer: Clive Champion; Photographer: Shania Shegedyn

282–283 (1) Designer: Sue Gillbanks; Photographer: Anton Curley; (2) Architect: Morehouse MacDonald & Associates; Photographer: Anton Curley

284–285 (1) Architect: Graham Pitts; Interior Designer: Sharon Cross; Photographer: Anton Curley; (2) Designer: Selina Tay, Collective Designs; Photographer: Peter Mealin; (3) Designer: Sandra Grummitt; Photographer: Chris Parker

286–287 (left) Architect: Thom Craig, Architecture Warren and Maloney; Photographer: Lloyd Park; (right) Designer: Kira Gray, Kitchens by Design; Photographer: Anton Curley

288–289 (1) (left) all color panels: Photo Essentials; (second from left) Architect: Gerard Murtagh; Photographer: David Sandison; (center) Photo Essentials; (second from right) Architect: Gabriel & Elizabeth Poole Design; Photographer: David Sandison; (right) Photo Essentials. (2) (left) all color panels: Photo Essentials; (second from left) Architect: James McCalligan, JMA Architects; Photographer: Tim Maloney (center) Photo Essentials; (second from right) Consultant: Jeff Tan, Unique Kitchen Fusion; Photographer: Peter Mealin; (right) Photo Essentials. (3) (left) all color panels: Photo Essentials; (second from left) Designer: Selina Tay, Collective Designs; Photographer: Peter Mealin; (center) Photo Essentials; (second from right) Veryan del Moro, Italy and Kitchens; Photographer: Anton Curley; (right) Photo Essentials. (4) (left) all color panels: Photo Essentials; (second from left) Designer: Darryl Gordon Design; Photographer: Simon Kenny; (center) Photo Essentials; (second from right) Architect: Paul Uhlmann; Photographer: David Sandison; (right) Photo Essentials.

290–291 (1) Architect: Michael Folk; Folk & Lichtman; Photographer: Simon Kenny; (2) Architect: Jonathan Waddy; Photographer: Paul McCredie; (3) Designer: Lynn Orloff-Wilson; Photographer: Simon Kenny

292–293 (1) Designer: Sandra Grummitt; Photographer: Chris Parker; (2) Architect: Darren Jessop, Jessop Townsend; Photographer: Anton Curley; (3) Architect: Bud Brannigan; Photographer: David Sandison

294–295 (1) Designer: Milvia Hannah, International Interiors; Photographer: Paul McCredie; (2) Designer: John Horvath, Hardy Interiors; Photographer: Simon Kenny; (3) Architect: Philip Follent; Philip Follent Architects; Photographer: David Sandison

296–297 (left) Architect: BHP Architects; Photographer: Shania Shegedyn; (right) Architect: Lindy Leuschke, Leuschke Group Architects; Photographer: Anton Curley

298–299 (1) Heather Menzies; (2) Architect: Chris Wilson; Wilson & Hill Architects; Photographer: Lloyd Park; (3) Architect: Steve McCracken and Richard Archibold, Architecture Warren & Maloney; Photographer: Anton Curley

300–301 (1) Image supplied by Winstone Wallboards and Park Terrace

Developments; (2) Heather Menzies; (3) Architect: Thom Craig, Architecture Warren & Maloney; Photographer: Lloyd Park

302–303 Architect: Richard Priest Architects; Photographer: Anton Curley

304–305 (1) Architect: Leo Campbell, Campbell, Luscombe Associates; Photographer: Simon Kenny; (2) Architect: Mark Sheldon, GSA; Photographer: Simon Kenny

306–307 (1) Image supplied by Firth Industries; (2) Architect: Karl Romandi, Karl Romandi & Helen DeLuis Architects; Designer: Michael Jan, Jan & Manton Design Architecture; Photographer: Simon Kenny

308–309 (1) Heather Menzies; (2) Architect: Shelly Gane, Cook Sargisson & Pirie; Photographer: Bruce Nicholson; (3) Architect: Craig Moller; Photographer: Bruce Nicholson

310–311 (1) Heather Menzies; (2) Image supplied by Radiant Heating; Photographer: Gérald Lopez